W9-ASJ-598

TWAYNE'S WORLD AUTHORS SERIES
A Survey of the World's Literature

SPAIN

Janet W. Diaz, Texas Tech University

EDITOR

The Spanish Pastoral Novel

TWAS 575

From an engraving in a seventeenth-century French translation of Lope de Vega's
Arcadia.

THE SPANISH
PASTORAL NOVEL

By AMADEU SOLÉ—LERIS

TWAYNE PUBLISHERS

A DIVISION OF G. K. HALL & CO., BOSTON

Published in 1980 by Twayne Publishers,
A Division of G. K. Hall & Co.
All Rights Reserved

Printed on permanent/durable acid-free paper and bound
in the United States of America

First Printing

Library of Congress Cataloging in Publication Data

Solé-Leris, Amadeu.
The Spanish pastoral novel.

(Twayne's world authors series ; TWAS 575 : Spain)
Bibliography: p. 161–67
Includes index.
1. Pastoral fiction, Spanish—History and criticism.
2. Spanish fiction—Classical period, 1500-1700—History
and criticism. I. Title.
PQ6147.P3S6   863'.03   79-24897
ISBN 0-8057-6417-8

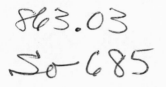

To the memory of
Roy Jones

Contents

About the Author

Amadeu Solé-Leris, a native of Catalonia, studied in Barcelona, Zurich and London. He graduated in Spanish and German at the University of London, where he subsequently taught Spanish language and literature at King's College. He is now an international civil servant in the United Nations system, but has maintained an active involvement in Hispanic studies, and is a member of the Association of Hispanists of Great Britain and Ireland. He specializes in the literature of the 15th and 16th centuries and has published studies on Montemayor, Gil Polo and Leone Ebreo, as well as *Los géneros dramáticos en las poéticas del Siglo de Oro* (London, 1974), a Spanish version of Margarete Newels' German original (Wiesbaden, 1959).

Preface

Spanish pastoral novels enjoyed a great vogue throughout Western Europe in the sixteenth and seventeenth centuries. As the pastoral genre as a whole—poetry, drama and prose—went into a decline in the eighteenth century, however, they retrospectively shared in the wholesale condemnation of pastoral which became increasingly common from the late 1700s onward. Both the Romantics and, later, the authors and critics imbued with views favoring Realism in art prevalent in the last century regularly denounced all traditional kinds of pastoral as false and artificial. A great novelist such as Pérez Galdós, (endowed with broad sympathies and a great degree of perception, but very much a man of his time) could refer to pastoral as "that ultimate degree of literary hypocrisy" [1] without the slightest qualm.

The banality of eighteenth-century versions of pastoral literature furnished plenty of justification for harsh judgments, and an equanimous assessment of the genuine qualities of earlier pastoral works remained virtually impossible for a long time. Even such a critic as H. A. Rennert, who expended so much effort in gathering essential data on *The Spanish Pastoral Romances* (1892, 1912) could hardly find a good word to say for the genre. Well into the twentieth century another respected scholar, W. A. Atkinson, was still producing a paper significantly entitled "Studies in Literary Decadence: The Pastoral Novel," [2] which begged the whole question by condemning the pastoral novel for failing to conform to standards irrelevant to it. The dismissive attitude dies hard. To this day, the mere word *pastoral* tends to suggest, to a certain type of mind, nothing but the preciosity of Watteau, or Marie Antoinette and her courtiers playing at shepherds in the gardens of Versailles—willfully remote from all reality, whether human, social, or spiritual. Even a comparatively recent major study on Italian, Spanish and French pastoral, Mia I. Gerhardt's *La Pastorale* (1950), while furnishing much valuable information, suffers from a "realistic" critical bias.

Yet, as each generation must reexamine the value judgments of its predecessors, a process of reassessment of the pastoral genre has been gaining momentum in the last few decades. For the genre as a whole, the English-speaking reader may consult especially the following (which, however, except for the precursor Greg, tend to pay scant attention to Spanish pastoral): W.W. Greg, *Pastoral Poetry and Pastoral Drama* (London, 1906); W. Empson, *Some Versions of Pastoral* (London, 1935; latest repr., London, 1968); R. Poggioli, various essays in 1957, 1959, 1963, collected in *The Oaten Flute—Essays on Pastoral Poetry and the Pastoral Ideal* (Cambridge, Mass., 1975); H. Levin, *The Myth of the Golden Age in the Renaissance* (Bloomington, 1969); Eleanor T. Lincoln, ed., *Pastoral and Romance: Modern Essays in Criticism* (New Jersey, 1969); P. V. Marinelli, *Pastoral* (London, 1971); H. E. Toliver, *Pastoral Forms and Attitudes* (Berkeley, 1971).

Serious revaluation of the Spanish pastoral novel began with López Estrada's edition of Montemayor's *Diana* (1946) and his critical study of Cervantes' *Galatea* (1948), together with Wardropper's epoch-making essay on Montemayor's novel (1951), Ferreres' edition of Gil Polo's novel (1953), Moreno Báez's further edition of Montemayor's (1955), and Avalle-Arce's fundamental *La novela pastoril española* (1959), which remains the standard work (in its updated 1974 edition).[3] These have been followed in the 1960s and 1970s by a good number of studies, the most useful of which will be referred to later, and are selectively listed in the Bibliography.

The present book is inspired by the belief that there is indeed much of value to be found in the Spanish pastoral novels. It does not, essentially, attempt to break new ground, but to produce a concise up-to-date survey in English which can, it is hoped, serve a dual purpose: adequately to inform the interested nonspecialist (even if he or she cannot read the texts in the original), and at the same time provide—within the exigencies of a brief format—a working basis of facts and critical comment from which students of Spanish literature may go on to delve more deeply into a worthwhile subject.

AMADEU SOLÉ-LERIS

Rome, Italy

Acknowledgments

My grateful thanks go to the staffs of the Biblioteca Nazionale, Rome, and of the British Library, London; the photocopying and interlibrary loan services of the Biblioteca Nacional, Madrid, and especially to Srta. María Oyarzun for unstinting assistance well beyond the line of duty; to my good friend and helpful bibliophile Sr. Joan Terrasa, and to Miss Maria Aloise for the impeccable typing of the manuscript.

Chronology

B.C.: 3rd century: Theocritus: Greek idylls.
3rd/2nd century: Moschus: Greek bucolic poems.
2nd century: Bion: Greek bucolic poems.
1st century: Virgil: Latin eclogues.

A.D.: 1st century: Calpurnius Siculus: Latin pastoral poems.
3rd century: Nemesianus of Carthage: Latin eclogues.
Longus: *Daphnis and Chloë* (Greek).
Heliodorus: *Aethiopica, or Theagenes and Chariclea* (Greek).
12th century: Metellus: *Bucolica Quirinalium* (1160).
Byzantine Greek romances: *Rhodanthe and Doricles, Drosilla and Charicles, Hysmenias and Hysmine*.

1265–1321 Dante: Latin eclogues on topical subjects (1319)

1304–1374 Petrarch: in Italian, *Canzoniere* (1360 and 1373); in Latin, *Bucolicum Carmen* (1346–48 and 1364).

1313–1375 Boccaccio: in Italian, *Il Filocolo* (c. 1336), *Ninfale d'Ameto* (1342), *Ninfale Fiesolano* (c. 1344); in Latin, *Bucolicum Carmen* (1351–66)

1398–1458 Marquess of Santillana: *serranillas* (c. 1420–40).

1433–1499 Marsilio Ficino: *Commentarium in Convivium Platonis de Amore* (written before 1474, published 1496). His own Italian translation: *Sopra lo amore o ver' convito de Platone* (before 1474, published posthumously, 1544).

1441–1494 Matteo Maria Boiardo: Eclogues in Latin and Italian.

1449–1492 Lorenzo de' Medici: Italian verse, including Petrarchan *Rime* and two eclogues (c. 1476–86).

c.1456–1530 Jacopo Sannazaro: in Italian, *Arcadia* (written 1480–96; incomplete ed. 1501; full ed. 1504); in Latin, five *Eclogae Piscatoriae* (before 1518).

c.1465–1537? Gil Vicente: dramatic eclogues, religious and secular.

1468?– 1530?	Juan del Encina: *Cancionero*, including dramatic eclogues (published 1496)
1474?– 1542	Lucas Fernández: *Farsas y églogas al modo pastoril* (published 1514).
c.1490– 1542	Juan Boscán: Spanish poems in Italian metres (from 1526).
1500	Pietro Bembo: *Gli Asolani*
1503– 1536	Garcilaso de la Vega: Three major verse eclogues (1533–1536). Sonnets and *canciones* in Italian metres.
1504	Sannazaro: *Arcadia* (1st complete edition).
1525	Mario Equicola: *Libro della natura d'amore*.
1528	Baldassare Castiglione: *Il Libro del Cortegiano*.
1530	Feliciano de Silva: *Amadis de Grecia*.
1532	Feliciano de Silva: *Don Florisel de Niquea*, I and II.
1534	Juan Boscán: *El Cortesano* (Spanish translation of Castiglione).
1535	Leone Ebreo (Judah Abarbanel): *Dialoghi d' amore* (written c.1501–1502) Feliciano de Silva: *Don Florisel de Niquea*, III.
1543	*Las obras de Boscán y algunas de Garcilaso de la Vega* (posthumous publication)
1547	Spanish translation of Sannazaro's *Arcadia* published (three other 16th-century translations remained in manuscript).
1549	Sannazaro's *Arcadia*: Spanish translation reprinted.
1551	Feliciano de Silva: *Don Florisel de Niquea*, IV.
1552	Alonso Núñez de Reinoso: *Los amores de Clareo y Florisea*.
1553	Antonio de Torquemada: *Coloquios satíricos*.
1554	Bernardim Ribeiro: *Menina e Moça*. (published posthumously).
1559?	Montemayor: *Los siete libros de la Diana*.
1563	Pérez: *Segunda parte de la Diana*.
1564	Gil Polo: *Primera parte de Diana enamorada*.
1565	Villegas: *Ausencia y soledad de amor* (in *Inventario*).
1568	First Spanish translation of Ebreo's *Dialoghi d'amore*, by Guedelha Yahia.
1573	Lofrasso: *Fortuna de Amor*.
1578	Sannazaro's *Arcadia*: third printing of Spanish translation.
1582	Gálvez de Montalvo: *El Pastor de Fílida*. Hurtado de Toledo: *El Teatro pastoril* (manuscript).

Chronology

1584   Second Spanish translation of Ebreo's *Dialoghi*, by Carlos Montesa.
1585   Cervantes: *Galatea*.
1586   López de Enciso: *Desengaño de celos*.
1587   González de Bobadilla: *Ninfas y pastores de Henares*.
1590   Third and best-known translation of Ebreo's *Dialoghi*, by "El Inca" Garcilaso de la Vega.
1591   Bernardo de la Vega: *El pastor de Iberia*.
1594   Covarrubias Herrera: *La enamorada Elisea*.
1598   Lope de Vega: *Arcadia*.
1599   Bartolomé Ponce: *Clara Diana a lo divino*.
1600   Mercader: *El Prado de Valencia*.
1607   Arze Solórzeno: *Tragedias de amor*.
1608   Balbuena: *Siglo de Oro*.
1609   Suárez de Figueroa: *La constante Amarilis*.
1612   Lope de Vega: *Pastores de Belén*.
1620   Espinel Adorno: *Los pastores de Sierra Bermeja*.
       Bramón: *Los sirgueros de la Virgen*.
1622   Botello: *El pastor de Clenarda*.
1624   Fernández Raya: *Esperanza engañada*.
1625   Enríquez de Zúñiga: *Amor con vista*.
1627   Tejeda: *Diana*
1629   Corral: *La Cintia de Aranjuez*.
1633   Conzalo de Saavedra: *Los pastores del Betis*.
1679   Ana· Abarca de Bolea: *Vigilia y octavario de San Juan Bautista*.

CHAPTER 1

Introduction: The Pastoral Tradition

I The Golden Age

THE pastoral novels that flourished in Spain for some hundred years from the middle of the sixteenth century were part of a much larger tradition. For something like two thousand years—dating from the idylls of Theocritus in the third century B.C. to, roughly, the end of the eighteenth century—the bucolic, or pastoral, myth was powerfully at work. Nor is its appeal dead today, couched though it may be in different terms. The traditional materials are simple enough, and have been described countless times: a peaceful landscape of meadows, brooks, fountains, and shady groves; in it, herdsmen devote the leisure afforded by their calling to singing of their love: its joys and, much more frequently, its sorrows (caused by the indifference, the absence, or the death of the beloved), and the beauty of their shepherdesses. Sometimes they muse alone, sometimes they vie with each other in song.

Love, nature, and (embodied in the shepherd's song) art: the tradition's vitality flowed from this fundamental triad, and from the multiplicity of relationships that each age could establish between its terms. Nature and the shepherd's (man's) place in it were of major importance in the universality of the tradition. This is why pastoral became the carrier of a closely related and even more powerful myth—that of the Golden Age, mankind's eternal dream of a place and time in which men led simple, innocent lives in harmony with a beneficent, gentle nature. As first formulated by Hesiod (and likewise in its Christian version, the garden of Eden), this paradise lay in the remote past. And the hope, implicit or formulated, that the paradise lost can somehow be regained, in some utopian future or in a life after death, has remained ever active in the human mind. Nowadays, the myth is embodied in different formulations, psychological mainly, and political: the world of archetypes, childhood as the age of

17

innocence and holistic experience, the millenium, and so on.[1] In its specifically pastoral form, it lost cogency with the rise of eighteenth-century rationalism and the new relationship to nature resulting from the sensibility of Romanticism. But during all those hundreds of years when it was an integral part of the common heritage, the atemporal pastoral world held up to the dwellers of the all-too-precarious real world, in countless works of art and literature, the bright image of its ideal landscapes and of its shepherds engrossed in the essentials of love, joy, sorrow, and death.

II *Theocritus and Virgil*

The main stages in the literary transmission of classical pastoral can be summarized briefly. Its origins are traced back to the *Bucolics* of Theocritus in the early decades of the third century B.C., though there is evidence of the existence before him of "artistic" pastoral poetry (as distinct from straight folksong) on the island of Cos, where he is known to have been a student. But Theocritus's poems were the first famous examples of the genre, and they established the basic themes and motifs. Set in the countryside of his native Sicily, but composed in the great city of Alexandria, under the patronage of its ruler Ptolemy Philadelphus, they also exemplify the characteristic pattern invariably repeated later on: pastoral poetry concerns supposedly simple countryfolk, but is written by and for the cultivated, highly refined dwellers of cities and courts. It embodies the sophisticate's longing for what is unspoiled. Hence the stylization inseparable from the genre. Theocritus, it is true, depicted many details of rustic life with a degree of realism, but this is hardly in evidence in his successors Moschus, also from Syracuse (flourished c. 150 B.C.), and Bion from Smyrna (dates very uncertain: third or second century B.C.).

Pastoral poems continued to be produced in the Hellenistic world, but it was with Virgil (70-19 B.C.) that pastoral acquired its definitive outline, as. it would be transmitted to later ages through the more accessible medium of Latin poetry. It would be difficult to overstate the importance of Virgil in the transmission of pastoral in European literature. In his ten *Eclogues* he brought together, in an exquisitely wrought array, the materials and motifs that were to nourish later pastoral. He also developed the device (only occasionally found in Theocritus) of referring to topical subjects, and contemporary characters, under pastoral cover. Above all, he invented Arcadia. The real Arcadia, wild and inaccessible in the rugged heartland of the Peloponnese, was as unfamiliar to him as to his readers. But its inhabitants were reputed (ever since Polybius) to lead simple, natural lives, and to be particularly skilled in music and song. A most suitable habitat, therefore, for the ideal homeland of pastoral after Sicily had become very much an unromantic, workaday part of the Roman empire. This was henceforth where shepherds would congregate for their songs, games, and discussions, at carefully selected spots—in flowery meadows, under trees, near water. From Virgil onward, the elements comprising this setting were recognized as forming a rhetorico-poetical topic, identified under the technical name of *locus amoenus*. This remained the main motif of nature descriptions well into the Renaissance and beyond.[2]

III *The Latin Eclogues of the Middle Ages and Early Renaissance*

Following Virgil, two names must be mentioned among the poets of the later Roman empire: Calpurnius the Sicilian (flourished c. A.D. 50), his first imitator, with seven Latin pastoral poems, and—clearly inspired by Calpurnius—Nemesianus of Carthage (flourished late third century A.D.), the author of four short *Eclogues*. There follows then a long succession of mostly obscure writers of Latin verse who, throughout the Middle Ages, cultivated the eclogue as an allegorical genre, in keeping with the medieval conception of Virgil as primarily an allegorical poet. The allegory was mostly religious. The Scriptures, from the lives of the patriarchs to the Adoration of the Shepherds, provided a ready framework of reference to pastoral life to encourage and justify the use of cognate materials from the classical tradition. Thus we see early Christian poets, such as Paulinus of Nola (c. A.D. 353–431), using elements from the pastoral tradition. Alcuin—i.e. Ealhwine—(735–804), ecclesiastic from York and learned adviser to Charlemagne, wrote allegorical pastorals. In 1160, a certain Metellus composed twelve *Bucolica* in honor of St. Quirinus, and so on. In the European Middle Ages, the pastoral terminology of the church became all pervasive; the Adoration of the Shepherds was one of the most popular subjects of the emerging drama, and Christ was, of course, the Good Shepherd. The ideal value of pastoral and its allegorical uses were thus part of every writer's background, mainly in a religious context.

From the beginning of the fourteenth century, however, Italian writers, ignoring the medieval Latin eclogues, were turning directly to classical sources for models. Petrarch and Boccaccio wrote Latin eclogues of Virgilian inspiration not only on religious but also on amorous and topical matters. The writing of such eclogues continued to be assiduously practiced throughout the fifteenth and well into the sixteenth centuries, their tone and subject matter becoming increasingly secular, mythological, and literary with the growing assimilation of the classical tradition. Leading humanists including Coluccio Salutati (1331–1406), Giovanni Pontano (c. 1426–1503), and Giovan Battista Spagnoli "Mantovano" (1448–1516) cultivated the writing of Latin eclogues, as did the Neapolitan Jacopo Sannazaro (c. 1456–1530), who was to create the first pastoral novel. Sannazaro, considered one of the best Latinists of his time, gave an original turn to Latin pastoral with his *Piscatoriae*, or piscatory eclogues, in which Arcadian shepherds are replaced by Neapolitan fishermen. He is credited with being the inventor of this adaptation of the traditional theme to a new setting, which was imitated by later writers both in Latin and in the vernacular.

IV *Italian Pastoral and the Greek Romances*

Meanwhile, the writing of classically inspired pastoral in Italian had also been developing. The first examples of this are found in Boccaccio's idylls and love romances, to which we shall return in a moment. In the fifteenth century, the focus for this development was the Florentine court of Lorenzo de'Medici, surnamed the Magnificent (1449–1492). Lorenzo's court was the center not only of the philosophical Neoplatonism that furnished the ideological foundation of Renaissance pastoral, but also of intense literary activity including experimentation with the writing of pastoral poetry in Italian. Lorenzo the Magnificent, himself a competent poet, set the example by writing two Italian eclogues with themes and motifs from Theocritus and Virgil. It was also in Florence that an anthology of *Bucoliche Elegantissime* was published in 1481 (and reprinted in 1494), including both some attempts at the genre by contemporary poets and the excellent, and widely influential, translation of Virgil's eclogues into Italian by Bernardo Pulci (1438–1488). Elsewhere in Italy, a major poet such as Boiardo (1441–1494; best known for his romantic epic *Orlando Innamorato*, which inspired Ariosto's famous sequel), had followed up the Latin eclogues of his youth with a series of ten eclogues in Italian, imitating Virgil's example even in the number of compositions.

It was in this context of growing acclimatization of pastoral to the Italian language and meters that Sannazaro produced what was to prove his most influential contribution to literature: *Arcadia*, an Italian pastoral romance in mixed prose and verse. Written mainly in the 1480s, and published in final form in 1504, *Arcadia* enjoyed at once a tremendous vogue, and became the recognized fountainhead of a version of pastoral which was to flourish first in Spain and then, largely through the example of Spanish practitioners, all over Europe for a good two centuries: the pastoral novel. The form, though virtually new, was not unprecedented; it had a remote forerunner in Longus' Greek romance of combined pastoral and adventure, *Daphnis and Chloe*, and models nearer home, as already mentioned, in some of Boccaccio's romances.

Daphnis and Chloe is one of a group of Greek prose romances of the late Hellenistic period that were an important source of materials for the Spanish pastoral novelists. Of uncertain date, all are believed to have been composed within the second and third centuries A.D. and can be regarded as the earliest examples of full-length novels in European literature.[3] They all combine, in generous doses, the two essential ingredients of love and adventure. The usual pattern is that of young lovers separated time and again by suspense-creating, mostly violent adventures and happily reunited in the end. The continuity of this genre was maintained in the literary culture of Byzantium, where there was a vigorous revival, with a spate of imitations, in the twelfth century. Some Greek romances were also known and appreciated, in the original or in Latin translations, in Western Europe (especially in Italy) throughout the Middle Ages.[4] It was, however, from the Renaissance onward that the Greek romances came into their own as models and sources of materials. One in particular, Heliodorus' *Ethiopian Story of Theagenes and Chariclea*, became immensely popular, setting the pattern and providing much material for novels of adventure in general as well as for the introduction of adventurous episodes into pastoral which, from the very beginning, was characteristic of Spanish pastoral novels: beginning *in medias res* with interventions of bandits and pirates, kidnappings, battles, storms at sea, surprising reversals of fortune, inset tales (where one of the characters tells his or her earlier adventures)—all serving the basic idea of true love emerging triumphant and purified from a series of trials. Among these works, *Daphnis and Chloe* is unusual in making rather less use of sensational incidents and giving central importance to the pastoral world in which its love story takes place, with idyllic nature descriptions and allusions to Theocritus and Virgil. It is, in all essentials, the first pastoral novel, although the possibilities of the genre thus invented by Longus were to remain virtually unexploited until the Renaissance. Boccaccio affected to hold the Greek romances in little esteem because they were "decked out with many lies" [5] but this did not preclude his making use of them when it suited his purpose. The *Filocolo*, for instance, includes material derived from several Greek romances, both early and twelfth century Byzantine, and a strong suggestion of *Daphnis and Chloe*.[6] Whatever Boccaccio's real views may have been on Greek romances, and on Longus' pastoral novel in particular, it is certain that, in his *Ameto*, he produced a work which, while religious and allegorical in intent, was in effect the first pastoral romance in a vernacular language. It became a model of great importance for the genesis of Sannazaro's *Arcadia*. Formally, *Ameto* set the pattern of combining prose and verse in a single work of fiction[7] which, with Sannazaro, became the consecrated form for the pastoral novel. It also offered the Neapolitan author a working example of the use of pastoral materials in a *locus amoenus* setting, with recounting of love stories, lyrical effusions, and plentiful mythological allusions. Another of Boccaccio's romances to which Sannazaro turned was the *Ninfale Fiesolano* which tells (all in verse, however, and with much material from Ovid) the story of a tragic love affair between a shepherd and a nymph, set in the Tuscan countryside.

V *Sannazaro's* Arcadia

The plot of Sannazaro's *Arcadia* is characteristically slender: Sincero (Sannazaro's poetic name), disappointed in love, has retired to Arcadia, where he shares the life of the shepherds. Eventually, a nymph leads him on a magic underground journey back to his native Naples, and he finds that his beloved has died in his absence. The novel opens with the author's *Proemio*, and closes with a *Farewell to the Rustic Flute*; the main body is structured in twelve sections of prose and twelve of verse, with a regular alternation *Prosa—Egloga*. These cover all aspects of life in pastoral Arcadia which became the standard elements of the later novels: idyllic nature descriptions (and especially beginning the first chapter with a *locus amoenus*); the rhythm of bucolic life (setting out with the flocks at dawn, gathering in shady spots, near water, during the heat of the day, returning to the village at dusk); songs by the shepherds, single or amoebaean (two shepherds singing alternate stanzas), mainly about love, but striking sometimes a rustic or burlesque note; the telling of past love stories by individual characters (a device subsequently much expanded by Spanish pastoral writers as a means of varying pace and subject matter); speeches and debates about love, poetry, and topics such as the praise of the Golden Age and denunciation of present times, the beauty and qualities of women, the secret properties of plants and stones, etc.; festivities and celebrations (such as the festival of Pales, goddess of flocks, and the visit to the temple of Pan); funeral rites; games and contests; magic, both black and white (the latter to heal the lovesick with spells), and supernatural interventions by gods and nymphs of classical mythology.

The book is written in the first person, i.e., as a literary elaboration of Sincero/Sannazaro's own unhappy love experience. In fact, Sincero's love story has been shown to follow literary models[8] very closely, so that the claim to be writing veiled autobiography is almost certainly more formal than genuine. (As we shall see, this also became part of the stock-in-trade of pastoral novelists. Spanish authors constantly claiming to be writing about events "that have truly happened.") Boccaccio was an important source, but by no means the only one. The presence of the other two great Italian masters, Petrarch and Dante, is also felt in *Arcadia*. But, above all, Sannazaro was steeped in the classical tradition and his novel has been described, not unfairly, as a mosaic of classical reminiscences.[9] Its texture is to a very large extent woven with classical materials, allusions, and reminiscences.

As might be expected, Theocritus and Virgil figure most prominently, but also Ovid (always important to writers on love, and an inexhaustible source of mythological lore); Horace and Tibullus (combining the themes of love and longing for rural life); Calpurnius, Nemesianus, and Longus; Hesiod, Strabo, and Pliny the Elder as sources of encyclopedic knowledge on natural sciences, agriculture, geography, history; and ideas, motifs, and turns of phrase culled from ancient authors dear to humanists: Homer and Anacreon; Cicero, Catullus, and Propertius; Lucan, Martial, and Juvenal; Ausonius and Boethius. Sannazaro's *Arcadia* was thus an eminently deliberate literary artifact, produced primarily for the delight of connoisseurs and fellow humanists (among whom it circulated in manuscript versions for years before appearing in printed form). A leading Neoplatonic scholar and poet such as Pietro Bembo (1470–1547), a friend of Sannazaro's, would thoroughly appreciate the mature assim-

ilation of classical culture that it represented, as well as the exquisite
skill with which it was wrought. Others (ladies, courtiers, the new
reading public of the bourgeoisie) less steeped in the literature of the
past but anxious to improve their minds and polish their taste, found
in the unobtrusive scholarship, delicate sensibility, and gentle
melancholy of *Arcadia* a most attractive means of doing so.

The universal dimension of the pastoral myth, activated once again
through Sannazaro's genuinely evocative poetic gift, appealed to
readers of all kinds. The result was a tremendous vogue. Reprints and
editions followed one another in quick succession. Within fifty years,
Arcadia had itself become a classic, being produced in scholarly
editions with extensive historical and philological commentaries.[10] In
establishing a form that encompassed both lyrical interludes and
scenes with action and dialogue, it opened the way for both the
pastoral drama and the pastoral novel. The drama flourished in Italy
with Tasso (*Aminta*, written 1573, published 1580) and Guarini (*Pastor Fido*, written 1583, definitive text published 1602) as its foremost
exponents. For the novel, it is now time to turn to Spain.

VI *Spain: The Italian Influence;*
Sentimental Novels and Romances of Chivalry;
Shepherd Plays; Pastoral Episodes

Throughout the sixteenth century, relations—political, military,
and cultural—between the Iberian and the Italian peninsulas were
close and continuous. The new Spanish monarchy of the Habsburgs
had inherited the traditional connection of the Crown of Aragon with
Italy, and was most active in maintaining important territorial interests (the Duchy of Milan, the Kingdom of Naples, Sardinia and
Sicily). Students,[11] soldiers, administrators, diplomats, priests and
prelates, scholars and poets, lawyers and merchants went ceaselessly
back and forth.[12] Cultural cross-fertilization was correspondingly
intense. To take the most striking example, highly relevant to the
spread of Renaissance pastoral poetry to Spain, the story has been
told many times of how, in the late 1520s, Juan Boscán (c. 1490–1542)
and Garcilaso de la Vega (1503–1536), the most profoundly influential
lyric poet of the century in Spain, successfully introduced hendecasyllabic verse from Italy into Spain, adapted Italian meters to
Spanish poetry, and thus began a poetic revolution. Spanish poets
discovered, or rediscovered, the poetry of Petrarch's *Canzoniere* and
of his Italian successors.

Their writing was quickly flooded with fresh imagery, especially nature imagery, and invigorated by the example of a poetic diction with a wider range of language, color, and texture than that of the courtly lyrics of their own native tradition.[13] Sannazaro was one of the more influential models.[14] In poetry, his Latin piscatorial eclogues, his Petrarchan *Rime* in Italian, and his *Arcadia* were fruitful sources for Garcilaso, especially in the three great verse eclogues which are his most important achievement, and for many others. In the field of prose, *Arcadia*, so popular already in its land of origin, could not fail to leave its imprint in a country like Spain where there existed at the time an extraordinary demand for prose fiction of all kinds. The late fifteenth-century sentimental novels of Juan de Flores (*Grisel y Mirabella* and *Grimalte y Gradissa*) and of Diego de San Pedro (*Amalte y Lucenda* and *La cárcel de amor*)[15] were still being busily reprinted and avidly read. The greatest vogue, however, during the first half of the sixteenth century, was that of the romances of chivalry: *Amadís de Gaula* (1508) and its myriad sequels. "They were published at an average rate of almost one a year between 1508 and 1550; nine were added between 1550 and the year of the Armada [1588]; only three more came out before the publication of *Don Quixote* [1605]." [16]

The drop after 1550 is revealing. Toward the end of that decade (probably in 1559), Jorge de Montemayor published his *Diana* and the Spanish pastoral novel came into existence. It became at once established as a new favorite form of fiction to which the reading public turned with eagerness. The initial impulse came from Sanna-zaro's *Arcadia*,[17] but Montemayor struck at once a distinctive note. The Spanish pastoral authors that followed modeled their works more often on Montemayor than on the Neapolitan author, though the prestige of *Arcadia*, as a stimulus and as a paradigm, remained unchallenged. As the scholar Reyes Cano sums it up, "*La Arcadia* played an important role in the evolution of Spanish pastoral books in the Golden Age, not so much as a direct model . . . but rather in its character as a consecrated work of literature regarded as a powerful stimulus to the bucolic ideal." [18] *Arcadia* was the crystallizing factor. The pastoral tradition already present in Spain, however, also made its own contribution to the new genre.

In Italy, pastoral poetry had developed as a deliberate taking-up of the heritage of antiquity. In Spain, on the other hand, as in France and in England, there had been throughout the Middle Ages an independent tradition in the use of pastoral elements in poetry and (as it developed from its religious, ritual origin) in the drama. In poetry, the *pastourelle* of Provençal troubadours had established the theme of the encounter between knight and shepherdess in a rustic setting, presented often in lighthearted rather than melancholy terms. This had been carried on in Spain in the *pastorelas* of Galician-Portuguese poetry of the twelfth and thirteenth centuries, and in the *serranillas* (mountain songs) of Castilian poets for the next two centuries.[19] In the drama, the shepherds of medieval Nativity and Easter plays and of rustic interludes in the moralities were, by the end of the fifteenth century, becoming the subject of brief independent pastoral plays, both secular and religious.[20] Juan del Encina (1468?–1530?), the creator of the modern Spanish drama; Lucas Fernández (1474?–1542), his lifelong rival; and the great bilingual Spanish-Portuguese playwright Gil Vicente (c. 1465–1537) wrote dramatic eclogues and pastoral *autos* (miracle plays) for performance at their patrons' courts.

The composition of *églogas representables* and their performance not only by professional actors but by ladies and courtiers as an exercise in amateur dramatics became very much the fashion. This is reflected in the pastoral novels, where verse eclogues are frequently performed by some of the characters in the course of festivities and celebrations. On the whole, however, the pastoral drama and the pastoral novel went their separate ways in sixteenth-century Spain, with very little interaction between the two. Nevertheless, the existence of a native tradition of pastoral poems and plays was in itself an important factor in preparing the ground for a ready reception of Renaissance pastoral, both as poetry, through Boscán and Garcilaso, and as fiction, with Sannazaro and Montemayor.

In the field of fiction, the full-blown pastoral novel had a number of forerunners, most notably in the form of pastoral episodes inserted in the romances of chivalry of Feliciano de Silva.[21] His *Amadís de Grecia* (1530) develops at length the story of Silvia, a high-born lady brought up as a shepherdess and courted by both a true shepherd and a knight turned shepherd for the sake of her love. In the four-book sequel to this romance, *Don Florisel de Niquea* (Parts I/II, 1532; Part III, 1535; Part IV, 1551) Silva not only continued, but greatly expanded the pastoral element. All the typical themes of the pastoral novel are already present here, as well as (in Part IV) the device of inserting a large proportion of love poems in the prose narrative, thus approaching very closely the characteristic prose-verse combination of the pastoral novel. A typical pastoral episode was also introduced by Silva in an entirely different, and also very popular, work of his, the *Segunda comedia de la famosa Celestina* (1534).

Feliciano de Silva may well be regarded as a key figure in the literary scene from which the Spanish pastoral novel was to emerge. The main impulse, no doubt, came to him from Sannazaro, but he was also familiar with the dramatic eclogues of Encina and Lucas Fernández, and in contact with the Portuguese writers of pastoral poetry Sá de Miranda (1481–1558) and Bernardim Ribeiro (1482?–1552). The former had played in Portugal the same role as Garcilaso in Spain in introducing the Italian poetic style and, with it, pastoral themes. Ribeiro, in addition to his verse eclogues, was the author of a sentimental novel, *Menina e Moça* (published posthumously in 1554), which contains important pastoral episodes. Another close friend both of Silva and of the Portuguese poets was Alonso Núñez de Reinoso (dates unknown), whose novel *Los amores de Clareo y Florisea* (1552, an imitation of Achilles Tatius' *Leucippe and Cleitophon* with added chivalric and pastoral episodes) brought together the strands of pastoral and the Greek romance. Although it is known that Montemayor entertained friendly personal relations with his fellow countryman Sá de Miranda and with Feliciano de Silva, the precise connection between him and this circle of writers who were actively concerned with pastoral has not been traced in detail. In any event, his *Diana* must be seen against the perspective of a growing involvement of Spanish and Portuguese writers with a classical, Italian pastoral ideal modified by native tradition.[22]

VII *Renaissance Neoplatonism and the Pastoral Novel*[23]

This pastoral ideal had been nourished by the Neoplatonic philosophy of the Italian Renaissance. It is no accident that Lorenzo the Magnificent, at whose court early attempts were made to write pastoral poetry in Italian, should also have been the patron, friend, and philosophical disciple of Marsilio Ficino (1433–1499), head of the Platonic Academy founded at Florence by Lorenzo's grandfather Cosimo the Great, and fountainhead of philosophical Neoplatonism.[24] Renaissance pastoral was thus, from the beginning, close to the roots of Neoplatonism. Naturally enough, the subject with which it dealt (love, and the longing for a state of pristine purity, symbolized by the Golden Age and its ideal landscapes) was central to the philosophy of Ficino and his followers. Pastoral poems and later pastoral novels illustrated in lyrical and fictional form the theoretical tenets of Neoplatonic love philosophy. The theory itself was largely disseminated through the medium of the so-called *trattati d'amore*,[25] a literary genre started by Ficino himself with *De Amore*, his Latin commentary on Plato's *Symposium* (written 1468–1469, published 1491).[26] These "treatises" usually took the form of debates between upholders of different views of love, culminating always in the demonstration of the rightness of the Neoplatonic philosophy.

The genre enjoyed great vogue in the sixteenth century. Its most influential examples (to which we shall return as we find their traces in the pastoral novels) were: Leone Ebreo's *Dialoghi d'amore* (written 1501–1503, published 1535)[27]; Pietro Bembo's *Gli Asolani* (1505); Mario Equicola's *Libro della natura d'amore* (1525),[28] and Baldassare Castiglione's phenomenally successful *Il Cortegiano* (written 1507, published 1528). The last one was not simply a treatise on love, but a complete handbook on "how to form a perfect courtier," i.e., the ideal Renaissance man, a model of balanced cultivation of character and faculties, taste and manners, that remained for centuries the European ideal of the gentleman. The book became at once immensely popular, swept through Europe,[29] and was one of the main channels through which Neoplatonic ideas flowed into sixteenth-century literature.

This is not the place to analyze Renaissance Neoplatonism. It must suffice to recall that its fundamental concept is the theory of emanations or hypostases, whereby the whole of Creation is seen as produced by successive emanations from the Godhead, or Absolute, down through a series of hierarchically arranged levels comprising, as main divisions, the intelligible world (or world of Ideas), the soul, and the corporeal world as perceived by the senses. This conception has two corollaries. One, that those levels that are closer to the Absolute have, by definition, a greater share of His nature than those farther away, hence the greater "reality" (in an absolute sense), goodness, and truth of the world of Ideas as compared to the sensible, corporeal world (which the uninitiated take for real). The second corollary is that every man's soul may, by contemplating increasingly "real," i.e., spiritual, kinds of beauty, rise from involvement in the sensible world, with its attendant suffering and inevitable disappointments, to serene contemplation of the Divinity (achieving thereby a kind of return to a spiritual Golden Age). Love, as Ficino had said, is "desire for beauty," but beauty is the splendor of the Good, and "the beauty of things is the lure by which the Soul of the lover is led to God." [30]

What this meant in practical terms is spelled out by Castiglione: the perfect courtier should love in such a way as to avoid the suffering usually associated with passion. This he achieves by rejecting the deceptive evidence of the senses, which would have him believe that beauty resides in the body, and by following the guidance of reason, which tells him that the body merely reflects the eternal beauty of God. The wise lover will therefore concentrate on loving the beauty of his lady's soul more solicitously than that of her body. He will then endeavor to rise from the direct contemplation of her beauty to that of its abstract essential image in his own mind, rising then still further from the love of particular to that of universal beauty, and so on, proceeding by successive steps until the ultimate mystical state of contemplation of the Divine Beauty is reached.[31] It is essential to this conception that all steps except the very last are guided by reason (they are, indeed, only possible under the guidance of reason). Reason is transcended only by mystical communion. This Neoplatonic ascent is often referred to as the "ladder" by which the soul returns to its origin. In this way the sharp division between the sensible world (imperfect and subject to change and decay) and the intelligible world (perfect, unchanging, everlasting) was bridged.

Next to love, the concept of nature was the other aspect of Neoplatonic philosophy of obvious major relevance to pastoral. The role of nature in Neoplatonic thinking reflects both the contrast between the sensible and the intelligible worlds, and the underlying continuity implied by the theory of emanations. On the one hand, nature is subject to the imperfections inherent in the sensible world. On the other, however, it is a clean reflection of the hypostatized divine beauty and goodness, untroubled by the self-willed disposition to make wrong choices which characterizes the human mind. It is, of course, this latter aspect that pastoral writers seized on: the *locus amoenus* becomes the visible manifestation of the Idea (which exists in the intelligible world) of a harmonious, beneficent nature, bathed in the bright light (a favorite Neoplatonic image) of the Beauty and Goodness irradiated by the Absolute. One thinks of the characteristic sparkling radiance of a painting such as the *Primavera* of Botticelli (c. 1445–1510), conceived and created in the atmosphere of Ficino's Platonic Academy.[32]

The relationship between man and this "visual representation of invisible archetypes" [33] is also two-edged. The shepherd pursuing his natural tasks in a Golden Age setting of simplicity and peace obviously makes his own contribution to the harmony of nature, which in turn merges in the grandiose harmony of the universe. But the turbulence of sensual desires clouds the lover's mind and impels him to pursue the lower, rather than the higher satisfaction, introducing a jarring discord, which can only be resolved by bringing the mind back (with or without supernatural aid) to a proper sense of values through the exercise of reason and self-discipline.[34] And there is yet another kind of relationship where man as artificer—*homo faber*—stands back from nature and competes with her, by the exercise of human skills, in the production of a different kind of beauty and harmony, more complex and more precarious. This animates the great debate of the sixteenth and seventeenth centuries on the relative merits and achievements of nature and art, a debate frequently reflected in the pastoral novels. It is against this ideological background (whose many other facets must be sacrificed here to the need for compression) that we shall have to examine the growth, success, and decline of the Spanish pastoral novel in the chapters that follow.

CHAPTER 2

Jorge de Montemayor: Los siete libros de la Diana
(*The Seven Books of Diana*)[1]

I *The Author*

JORGE de Montemayor (c. 1520–1561/62) was born in Montemôr-o-Velho, near Coimbra, in Portugal. His father was a silversmith, and his ancestry may have been Jewish. His family name is unknown, the surname he always used being simply a Castilianized version of his birthplace. He was a professional musician and served in this capacity, and later in other positions, in the households of Princess Maria of Austria (eldest daughter of the Emperor Charles V) and of her sister Princess Joanna (later Princess of Portugal). In 1554 he may have travelled to England and Flanders in Prince Philip's retinue. He took part in the 1556-59 wars against the French in Flanders, returned to Spain, and spent some time in Valencia. He was killed by a jealous friend over a love affair in Piedmont (Northern Italy) sometime in 1561 or 1562.[2]

The bulk of Montemayor's poetic output is contained in *Las obras de George de Montemayor, repartidas en dos libros* (Antwerp, 1554), a volume of collected poems, in two parts, one of secular—mainly amatory—and one of religious verse. In 1559, Montemayor's poems were included in the Index of the Inquisition, but the interdiction was soon lifted from the secular works, which were being reissued in 1562. The first edition of *Diana* is undated, but was published in Valencia in or shortly before 1559.[3] His translation of Catalan poems by the Valencian poet Ausiás March (1397?-1458) was also published in Valencia, in 1560. Montemayor wrote exclusively in Spanish (with minor exceptions such as some Portuguese dialogue in the scenes set in his own home valley of the river Mondego in Book VII of *Diana*).

Montemayor brought to literature little of the learned cultural equipment so conspicuous in his model Sannazaro. It seems certain that he knew neither Latin nor Greek, and his knowledge of classical history and mythology—essential at a time when all writing was (and was expected to be) liberally sprinkled with classical allusions—was, to say the least, shaky.[4] Yet his literary achievements won him public applause and the respect of fellow writers and critics, who admired his natural disposition.[5] He was well connected with authors in Spain and in Portugal, including some who, like Sá de Miranda and Feliciano de Silva, were important for the transmission of pastoral.

II   *The Novel*

Argument (summarizing previous events): "In the fields of the auncient and principall citie of *Leon* in Spaine, lying along the bankes of the river *Ezla*, lived a Shepherdesse called *Diana*, whose beautie was most soveraigne above all others in her time."[6] She was loved by Sireno and Silvano, and reciprocated the former's affections. Yet, during her lover's prolonged absence she had married Delio, a wealthy shepherd.

Book I: Sireno's return and his grief at Diana's marriage. By the alder-tree fountain, he and Silvano comment on her present unhappiness with disagreeable, uncouth Delio. Arrival of Selvagia, also nursing a broken heart. Conversation on inconstancy in love. *Selvagia's tale*: She tells of her own tragicomic love-tangle, involving mistaken identities, both sexual and personal (she had fallen in love with Ismenia, believing her to be Alanio in woman's dress), and shifting attachments (three of the four main characters change allegiances at least once), resulting in frustration all around: Selvagia loved Alanio, who pined for Ismenia, who pursued Montano, who—closing the circle—doted upon Selvagia.

Book II: Next morning, again by the fountain, Selvagia, Sireno, and Silvano spy upon three nymphs, one of whom describes Diana's and Sireno's former love and tender farewell. Three armed wild men try to seize the nymphs. The shepherds rush to their assistance but are about to be overwhelmed when a mysterious lady, Felismena, in pastoral dress but fully armed, intervenes and kills the attackers. *Felismena's tale* is not pastoral, but a story of love and intrigue, in realistic urban settings, based on an Italian *novella* (and was to inspire the main plot in Shakespeare's *Two Gentlemen of Verona*).[7] Felismena (fated at birth, together with her twin brother, to be lucky at arms and unlucky in love) had followed her fickle lover Don Felis from Seville to the Court, disguising herself as a man for secrecy. She had been taken on as a page ("Valerio") by unsuspecting Don Felis, and used as go-between to his new love, Celia. The latter, however, spurned the nobleman's advances and fell in love with the "page," dying of a broken heart in consequence. Felis left in despair, and Felismena has been looking for him ever since. The nymphs now propose that all should accompany them to their mistress Felicia, high priestess of the goddess Diana and a wise sorceress "whose exercise is to remedy the passions of love."

Book III: As night falls, the company come upon Belisa sorrowing on a river island. *Belisa's tale* is set in a Castilian farming village. Arsenio, a wealthy widower, had been courting Belisa with the help of his son Arsileo, who wrote poems and love letters for him. Belisa, realizing where the true authorship lay, had fallen in love with the son. Arsenio, coming unawares upon the young lovers, had killed his son, unrecognized, in a passion of jealousy, then committed suicide. Belisa had run away in despair, to await her own death in solitude.

Book IV: The wanderers, now joined by Belisa, reach Felicia's temple-palace, in a beautiful natural setting. They are shown its beauties (marble fountain, monument to Mars, Hall of Chastity, Hall of Diana, garden cemetery of chaste nymphs and ladies), and listen to Orpheus' song in praise of Spanish ladies. There is lavish entertainment and a philosophical conversation on the nature of love. [Interpolation: *Tale of Abindarráez and the beautiful Jarifa*[8]].

Book V: Next morning, Sireno, Selvagia, and Silvano drink Felicia's potions. After a magic sleep, Selvagia and Silvano find that their former attachments have been replaced by a powerful mutual love. Sireno's potion obliterates his love for Diana, leaving him in a state of contented detachment. Felismena sets out again on her quest (of which Felicia has predicted the happy outcome), and the healed shepherds return home while Belisa remains with Felicia. Felismena meets Belisa's supposedly dead Arsileo, who is relating his tale to Amarílida: neither he nor his father are dead, and the scene witnessed by Belisa had been a magic deception practiced upon her by malicious Alfeo, the village sorcerer. Felismena directs Arsileo to Felicia's palace. Back in the village, Sireno, Silvano, and Selvagia meet Diana (who appears now in person for the first time). She is shocked at Sireno's indifference, recalls her former happiness with him, and complains of her husband's jealous disposition. Meanwhile, Arsileo and Belisa are reunited in Felicia's palace.

Book VI: Felismena patches up a lovers' quarrel between Amarílida and Filemón, and travels on. In Diana's village, she and Sireno argue about past rights and wrongs. He is moved, but only momentarily, by the sight of her familiar flock. He and Silvano sing of their past love for Diana. She departs weeping.

Book VII: In the meadows of the Mondego valley in Portugal, with the city of Coimbra and Montemayor's birthplace, Montemôr-o-Velho, in the distance, Felismena witnesses Danteo's unsuccessful wooing of Duarda (the dialogue is in Portuguese). She also rescues a wounded knight, Don Felis, from his attackers. A potion of Felicia's, brought by a nymph, heals his wounds and restores his original love. The novel ends with a triple wedding at Felicia's palace (Felismena/Felis, Belisa/Arsileo, Selvagia/Silvano), and the announcement of a sequel.

III   Structure: The Plot and the Characters

Since B. W. Wardropper's basic study,[9] it has become commonplace to point to the structural symmetry of *Diana*. Books I to III introduce the characters and their love problems. Selvagia (Book I), Felismena (Book II), and Belisa (Book III) are successively added to the central thread of the Sireno-Silvano-Diana situation. At the same time, the appearance of the nymphs, whose episode with the wild men, apart from introducing some action by way of contrast, has an ideological point (see below), begins a dynamic process: the growing company of sorrowful lovers embarks upon a quest, to seek relief through Felicia's healing powers.[10] Book IV is both the turning point of the plot (Felicia promises a happy outcome to everyone's problems) and its intellectual core (discussions on the nature and effects of love). Books V to VII describe the working out of the solutions: there are changes of heart and reunions, and the company of lovers scatters (to be reunited, however, for the final marriage festivities). The brief introduction of two new pairs of lovers (Amarílida/Filemón and Duarda/Danteo) paves the way for the never-to-be-written sequel.

The idea of a quest suggests happenings and adventures. Significantly, the two episodes of violent action are placed at the beginning of the lovers' quest (when the wild men attack the nymphs) and at the end, when the last member of the original company, Felismena, achieves her heart's desire. Yet in spite of these episodes, and of the variety resulting from much lively matter contained in the characters' tales, a large proportion of *Diana* is given over to the expression and analysis of sentiments in the context of different lover-beloved relationships. The bulk of the book consists of discussions and lyrical effusions in prose and verse on the subject of love, and descriptions of its psychological effects.

The summary of previous events which opens *Diana* claims that the book contains "diverse histories of accidents, that have truly happened, though they go muffled under pastorall names and style," [11] and in Montemayor's own time it was thought that the model for Diana was a certain Anna of Valencia de Don Juan, in the valley of the river Ezla, near León. Anna was still alive, aged, we are told, about sixty, in 1602, when King Philip III and his queen, while travelling in that region, made a point of meeting her "because she was so famous and had been so greatly praised by Jorge de Montemayor in his story and poems." [12]

As nothing whatsoever is known, however, about this lady or about the circumstances of the relationship, it is perfectly useless to speculate about the autobiographical content of the novel. It is also irrelevant to the consideration of *Diana* as a work of literature, for autobiographical involvement bears no relation to literary worth. It is, on the other hand, highly relevant to recall that the claim that real characters are being portrayed in shepherd's disguise is as old as Virgil's *Bucolics*, and that Sincero, the protagonist of Sannazaro's *Arcadia*, is explicitly autobiographical. Montemayor's statement may therefore reasonably be regarded (whatever its actual substance) as no more than an expected gesture within the convention in which he had chosen to write.

What is important is that *Diana* stands before us as the forerunner of the modern psychological novel. At first sight, the treatment of the characters tends to strike the modern reader as stereotyped. They are, until Felicia's intervention, unswervingly faithful (e.g. Sireno, Silvano, Selvagia, Felismena, Belisa) or excessively fickle (e.g., Diana, all the characters in Selvagia's tale except herself, Don Felis). Their love is either requited or unrequited, without intermediate nuances—mostly unrequited, or requited only temporarily by one of the inconstant partners.

We must not, however, expect from Montemayor something he did not set out to do. His aim was not to perform the kind of complex exploration of highly individualized characters in a real social context which Cervantes was to achieve so triumphantly some half a century later in *Don Quixote*. Montemayor's purpose was to study human beings functioning *purely* as lovers, i.e., unhampered and undistracted by social, economic, or other considerations. By means of the experiment thus conducted under controlled conditions, he examined the operation of three key factors enumerated in the first sentence of Book I, "Love, Fortune and Time," and drew some conclusions of general validity about love and lovers. This means, of course, that he was deliberately dealing with types, rather than with individuals.

Granted this approach, however, what is striking is the amount of individual characterization actually to be found in *Diana*. Montemayor had a novelist's flair for keen observation and the telling detail, and used it to good purpose to enhance the liveliness of his story at many points. Thus we have the carefully graded nuances of the scene where Selvagia originally meets Ismenia, develops an attachment for her as a woman, because of her great beauty, then an even greater one—because it can now be reinforced by acknowledged sexuality—when she is deceived into believing Ismenia is a man. Or there is Belisa's curious but all too human predicament of loving the son but not managing to get herself to the point of discouraging the father's lavish courting; as she herself confesses: "as love increased with the son, so did fondness for the father," though she takes care to make the difference clear: "though it was not all of the same quality." At any rate, this gave her no occasion "to show disfavour [to the father] or to refuse his presents." In Diana's case, note her annoyance at finding that Sireno, the lover she had deserted, is no longer heartbroken: "for God knows she would rather have heard his wonted complaints than be compelled to believe in his new liberty." And she regrets Silvano's disaffection even more than Sireno's because Silvano has thereby found happiness while Sireno, at least, is merely indifferent. Or, finally, the scene in which Sireno, Selvagia, and Diana gingerly test the new relationship: the two shepherds lightly flirting with Diana, who struggles to conceal her distress, while Selvagia watches uneasily, wondering how sure she can be of Silvano's love, yet carefully refraining from any intervention that might precipitate unwelcome developments. This is a scene such as Montemayor would often have witnessed at court: a light bantering tone masking undercurrents of shifting, precarious personal relationships. On the whole, however, the characters in *Diana* are primarily the means whereby Montemayor illustrates in an artistic medium an essentially theoretical consideration of the scope and significance of love. The most fruitful approach to an appreciation of *Diana* is through an understanding of the underlying ideology.

IV   The Ideas: Theory of Love; The Pursuit of Beauty;
The Wild Men; Time and the Magic Potion

Renaissance theories of love, as developed in Italy from Ficino onwards, furnished the intellectual nourishment on which the pastoral novel grew. Montemayor turned to Leone Ebreo for the required Neoplatonic philosophical stiffening. Book IV, the pivotal section of *Diana*, ends with a philosophical debate on love and its relationship to reason which is almost a literal translation of a passage in the *Dialoghi d'amore*. But, for all that he was writing a pastoral in a "modern" mode, the root of Montemayor's thinking lay in the fifteenth century: and he selected accordingly from his source to produce what was, fundamentally, a traditional medieval view.

Briefly,[13] Montemayor follows Ebreo in drawing the standard distinction between good love (*buen amor* or *amor honesto*) and false love (*falso amor* or *amor deshonesto*). The latter springs from "a base and dishonest appetite" and unreasoningly pursues physical satisfaction (as exemplified by the wild men's attack on the nymphs). *Buen amor* is born of reason (for love is preceded by knowledge of the beauty—physical and spiritual—of its object), but is not subject to its control, and aims at spiritual union with the beloved. In both cases, the nature of the resulting state of mind is equally passionate and beyond the control of reason. Here Montemayor parts company with Ebreo. The philosopher could not overlook a basic difficulty: if pure love is as irrational as the other kind (the difference lying only in the aim pursued), how can it claim to be the most perfect spiritual experience while excluding the power of reason, man's highest gift, and that which distinguishes him from animals? So Ebreo had to develop the theory of the two kinds of reason: *ordinary reason*, concerned with the proper ordering of normal human affairs, cannot control love. But over and above it there exists an *extraordinary reason*, the purpose of which is to pursue a higher good, embodied in the beloved, even though it means sacrificing those things that men otherwise hold dear. The Renaissance Neoplatonist has to insist on the necessary, positive connection between love and reason at all stages short of mystical union with God. But for Montemayor (as repeatedly stressed in the novel) reason is always overcome by love. And love is a doom against which it is useless to struggle. Fate is everything, man's will nothing. The lover is subject to love, and the course of love is subject to fortune. But fortune is notoriously unstable, and love cannot but be equally so. The ideal proclaimed is, of course, constancy, but fickleness is portrayed again and again as the most current, normal human condition. *Diana* can, not unfairly, be described as a study in the impermanence of human attachments.

If love has complete mastery over heart and mind, it follows that the lover's loyalty will shift with the vagaries of a passion attracted now by one, now by another beautiful human being, and subject to the ups and downs of fortune. Jealousy and suffering are inseparable from love—jealousy, because it is its natural consequence; suffering, because it ennobles the lover: "they that suffer more are ever best" says Montemayor. The fatalistic acceptance of the power of love, seen as not amenable to the exercise of reason or free will, and the approval of jealousy and suffering are the hallmarks of the characteristic conception of medieval courtly love. This conception had inspired, even as the Middle Ages were waning, the vast amount of courtly lyric in the Spanish *Cancioneros* of the fifteenth century, and retained much of its vitality through the first half of the sixteenth. [14] Alongside the new lyric in Italianate meters, copious amounts of traditional *Cancionero* poetry continued to be written, published, and read; not least by Montemayor himself.

In his novel, Montemayor sticks to this fifteenth-century view. Yet he does not propound a purely traditional attitude. His shepherds pursue and achieve marriage as a legitimate aim. There is an unresolved dichotomy in Montemayor between the belief that "they that suffer more are ever best" and the explicit approval of fulfillment in marriage. He was poised between the courtly love of earlier ages and the more positive attitude of the Neoplatonists who, while seeing human love only as a step toward divine love, did not on that account necessarily despise its reasonable fulfillment.

Beauty is of paramount importance in the Neoplatonic scheme of things, and the beauties of nature are of course an essential ingredient of the pastoral tradition. Montemayor's novel, nourished by both, is pervaded by a strong sense of universal beauty. Nature descriptions are skillfully wrought to convey a sense of beauty, peace, and harmony. And the human beauty of the characters, through the passions it inspires, is the mainspring of every action.

It is in this light that the sexual ambiguity must be seen in the two episodes where one woman falls in love with another, believing her to be a man (Selvagia and Ismenia/Alanio in Book I, and Celia and Felismena/Valerio in Book II). Selvagia's and Celia's instincts give them no warning of the true sexual nature of the other person, precisely because the attraction is portrayed as being, fundamentally, *good love*, the Neoplatonist's love of beauty: to see beauty is to desire it, in a spiritual sense, wherever it may be found. To what extent this is so is highlighted by the way in which Selvagia's attachment begins. She is powerfully attracted to Ismenia—when first meeting her as a woman—by the beauty of her eyes and hands. There follows a love declaration that is in no way different from that which a male wooer would address to his lady: "fair and gracious shepherdess," says Selvagia, "it is not only this hand [her own, which Ismenia has taken in hers] which is always ready to serve you, but also the heart and thoughts of her to whom it belongs." She then proceeds, still *before* being deceived into thinking she is dealing with a man, ardently to entreat the other shepherdess to show her the full beauty of her hitherto muffled face, exactly as a love-struck shepherd or courtier, would.

Of course, the woman-in-man's-disguise device occurs frequently in the literature of the time, and we must beware of treating with undue solemnity these two episodes, which Montemayor handles lightly and uses for good functional purposes. One of them illustrates Ismenia's malicious, heartless playfulness, and the other Felismena's selfless devotion to her inconstant lover. In both cases, Montemayor is playing the ambiguity for what it is worth to interest and amuse his readers. But he is also, at a more serious level, demonstrating the implications of Neoplatonic love theory.

The episode of the wild men, which has puzzled some critics, or has been regarded simply as an element of aesthetic contrast by others, also falls into place when considered from the viewpoint of Neoplatonic love theory. The attack on the nymphs, which might appear to jar in the peaceful context of pastoral, serves, in fact, to exemplify the disruptive effect of *false love*, i.e., of the sensual desire which is at the opposite pole of the ennobling sentiment that moves the Neoplatonic lover. This desire is concerned only with physical satisfaction and will not hesitate to use violence to achieve it. Such violence, as Avalle-Arce pointed out in an illuminating analysis of the whole episode,[15] shatters the universal harmony of nature (of which man is a part) postulated by Neoplatonism. These three living embodiments of *false love* complete the range of love cases in *Diana*: to the examples of constant or inconstant but always "honest" and chaste lovers, seeking fulfillment in marriage, are now added specimens of "false," bestial lovers.

Love's arising, as has been seen, is subject to fate. Its extinction is dependent on both fate and the passage of time, as we can learn from an instructive exchange early in Book II: "Silvano said sighing:'Do you perhaps know any [remedy for our suffering]?' Selvagia answered: 'Most certainly I do. And you know what, shepherd? To leave off loving,' 'And could you bring yourself to this?' said Silvano. 'If fortune and time so ordained' replied Selvagia." Time is of central significance in *Diana*. " 'Amor, la fortuna, el tiempo' are indivisible aspects of the same entity, which is life lived in time." As soon as passion breaks in upon their existence, lovers experience a "new and anguished awareness of the passage of time," and ponder "las mudanças de los tiempos." Time "is the destroyer of happiness, but it is also the healer of wounds." [16]

The note is sounded at once in the *Argument*: during Sireno's enforced absence, "time and Diana's heart were changed." Subsequently, the three nymphs, recalling Diana's affecting leave-taking from Sireno, marvel at "how time had cured her grief, which seemed at their farewell to be without remedy." Diana herself tartly comments on Sireno's change that "time heals infinite things which seem incurable to men." This is a clear pointer to the meaning of the magic potion[17] administered to Sireno by Felicia. Sireno has been healed by time, i.e., the brief period of unconsciousness induced by the magic water is equivalent to the accelerated passage of time, and the magic lies only in the speeding up.

The key passage closing the theoretical discussion on love at the end of Book IV, where Montemayor leaves aside Leone Ebreo to put forward his own unaided views, makes the point very clear. The question is: why does love, in most cases, grow cold through absence? The answer is that, in the absence of the beloved, the amorous passion can only continue to feed on memory. Memory displays its contents to the understanding, which moves the will, which in turn generates desire to see the absent beloved, and a corresponding sense of deprivation. But, as time passes, memory gradually loses its strength and vigor; and so does the love that depends on it through the other powers of the soul. "And to think" concludes Cinthia the nymph, addressing Belisa, "that time would not heal your grief if you left the remedy thereof in the hands of wise Felicia, is to be greatly mistaken." Upon which Felicia comments: "It would be no small cruelty in me to leave the remedy of one who needs it so badly to such a leisurely agent as time is." While some people recover from their broken hearts quite quickly, truly constant lovers take so long to be healed by time that their grief may outlast their lifespan. Which is, of course, why Felicia resorts to the magic water to accelerate the process.

Worth noting is how neatly this explanation links both categories of lovers—the constant and the fickle. It is simply a matter of time—if the change of heart occurs rapidly, the lover is fickle; if it takes a very long time to accomplish, he—or she—is constant. It is curious that Montemayor should have taken such trouble to point to the meaning of the magic water, yet been upbraided ever since for introducing an extraneous, mechanical element to effect the turning point of the novel's plot, beginning with Cervantes. In the often-quoted passage of the burning of Don Quixote's library by the curate and the barber (Part I, ch. 6), Cervantes praises *Diana* as a whole but sternly demands that everything relating to Lady Felicia and the magic water should be expunged therefrom. Only very recently has the true meaning of the magic potion been properly identified.[18]

Yet the misreading of this crucial point is not merely due to the inattention of generations of readers. Against the background of novels of chivalry and of adventure, where magical devices were common currency and carried no significance beyond that of providing excitement and suspense, it was a point that needed to be made more explicitly if the magic potion was to stand out as something different. For different it certainly is. By symbolizing the effects of the passage of time on the lovers' psyche it draws attention to the dynamic nature of human character. It serves not only the mechanical purpose of advancing the plot, but it is functional, however cursorily, in terms of the changes certain characters undergo as a consequence of their experiences and the passage of time. In this sense, it can also be seen as a symbol of a new approach adumbrated in Montemayor's novel—the beginnings of a move toward the portrayal and analysis of character development typical of the later psychological novel. We shall see, in the corresponding chapters, that the major pastoral novels which followed (Gil Polo, Cervantes, Lope de Vega) were to carry this process several steps farther.

V *Literary Form and Technique: Narrative and Lyricism; Description (Idea, Nature, and Supernature); Music and Clothes*

Montemayor took the narrative devices of the adventure story and the Italian *novella* and blended them with the lyrical quality of traditional pastoral to produce, in C. B. Johnson's apt phrase, a

"novel pastoral." Since he was primarily concerned with the exploration of lovers' states of mind, it is not surprising that Montemayor
should have placed the emphasis on the lyrical aspect. Narration,
accordingly, serves the purposes of lyricism. Felismena's tale is a
particularly good example of this; its considerable narrative interest is
closely blended with the lyrical expression of the heroine's emotions
as she tells her story.

C. B. Johnson has shown how skillfully Montemayor employs
devices for creating and sustaining narrative tension while serving
the primary purpose of furthering a fundamentally lyrical interest.
The vogue of *Diana* throughout the sixteenth century shows that
Montemayor's new blend exactly suited the taste of the time. Later
critics, on the other hand, have frequently complained of the static
character of the novel. Its pace is certainly leisurely. There is no
dearth of events, but these are disposed of briefly (witness the wild
men's episode which takes up barely two pages), while the flow stops
at every turn to allow for lyrical effusions in the form of songs,
dialogues and monologues, the lyrically accented telling of characters' past histories, and the descriptions of natural and (in the case of
Felicia's palace) supernatural settings.

Traditionally, nature descriptions in pastoral are of the most general kind—in our terms, it is an ideal, not an actual landscape that is
being depicted. Hence a high degree of abstraction prevails. Montemayor's pastoral settings are no exception: green meadows, shady
groves, clear fountains, fair river banks. Each noun is regularly
qualified by the same epithet so that they become one single semantic
unit operating practically as a symbol. The adjectives simply bring
out the pleasing, peaceful aspects of nature, but add no particulariz-
ing touch (flowers, to give a further example, are "fresh and fragrant"
or occasionally "golden"). Two of them, however, are used more
freely, to heighten the atmosphere of peace and beauty: "fair" (which
also qualifies, for instance, valleys, or groves as well as rivers), and
"delightful." It is a narrow range, yet handled with Montemayor's
skill, it is surprisingly effective in creating an atmosphere of peace,
harmony, and natural beauty.[19]

The description of human beauty is similarly abstract. It goes even
further so that, with very few exceptions, description is hardly the
right term for it. The women in *Diana* are simply beautiful, without
qualification. Thus, all we are told about Selvagia's beauty on her first
appearance is "that it was not little"; Felismena is defined as being "of
such great beauty and disposition"; and even Diana, when we at last

meet her in Book V, is seen merely "with such great beauty." [20] There is, however, one symbol of supreme womanly beauty: "golden hair." She of whom this is predicated is thereby, with no need for further details, identified as a paragon of beauty. In most cases, this is quite literally the only thing we are told about a shepherdess' or nymph's beauty. That this was consciously used as a symbol, and need not by any means be literally true, is brought out very clearly in Danteo's pleading with Duarda in the Portuguese episode, when he refers to her "golden hair" which we had been told, in the realistic description of a few pages earlier, was "not very blond." This abstract quality of the ideal pastoral world is of course one of the things that modern readers had difficulty in coming to terms with, as long as nineteenth-century ideas of "realism" prevailed. For a proper appreciation it is therefore essential not to lose sight of the fact that the Neoplatonic view of the matter was exactly the opposite: ultimate reality resided in the world of ideas, of which the material world around us was but an imperfect reflection.

The Arcadia of the classical pastoral tradition existed beyond place and time. Sannazaro himself, though his Sincero came to Arcadia from his native Naples and returned to it at the end, had been careful not to detract in any way from the pure ideality of the pastoral world. Montemayor, on the other hand, adopts a novel approach there, too. His pastoral world, as we have seen, meets all the ideal requirements but is nevertheless explicitly set on the banks of the Ezla river, not far from the city of León. Other references to actual locations abound. [21] Montemayor's ideal world is thus firmly related to the real geography of the Iberian peninsula, and pastoral is brought one step closer to the world of everyday reality.

There are two other worlds—in addition to the ideal pastoral setting—where things happen in *Diana*: the supernatural world of Felicia and her palace, and the realistic natural world of Felismena's tale and of the Portuguese episode in Book VII (and, for all that a magician is introduced for the sake of a surprise ending, also of Belisa's tale, set in a prosperous agricultural community of Castile). The novel thus operates at three different levels of reality, and Montemayor uses two distinct descriptive modes in dealing with them: abstract and general for the ideal level, detailed and concrete for the other two, with the difference that, in the supernatural world, the objects or scenes described are, as might be expected, fantastic in themselves, while in the natural world of everyday experience, they are wholly realistic.

Descriptive detail is at its most realistic and specific in dealing with the supernatural world (it being a well-tried literary device to add to the credibility of unlikely matters by describing them in circumstantial detail). A glance at the description of Felicia's palace and of the festivities taking place therein is enough to confirm this. The specificity of plant species and building materials in the palace cemetery, for example, stands in striking contrast to the generality observed in the ideal landscapes: in the space of only eight lines we have ivy, myrtle (mentioned both by its popular and its learned names: "arrayán" and "mirto"), grapevine, jasmine, and honeysuckle, growing around and over fountains made of alabaster, veined marble, and metal.

In the realistic scenes of the natural world, the degree of detail varies. In the description of natural landscapes and urban scenes, the setting is successfully conveyed with a minimum of realistic touches revealing careful observation and a fine sensibility. The classic passage for this is the description of Montemayor's own native river valley which opens Book VII, including a splendidly conveyed observation of ripening grain swaying in the wind, of which it has been claimed with considerable justification that it set once and for all the tone of descriptive prose in Spanish literature.[22] The incidents of Felismena's tale (Don Felis' nocturnal serenades to his new lady love; the bustle of ladies, courtiers, pages, and servants at court; the kinds of love affairs open to an enterprising young page) all witness Montemayor's ability to draw on the observed reality of scenes with which his life as a courtier had made him abundantly familiar.

The characters of the natural world are introduced in concrete detail. Their names are current ones; their appearance, language, mentality, and occupations correspond to their actual position. Duarda, the Portuguese shepherdess, rejects her suitor Danteo in down-to-earth language. She and her friend Armia are described in more detail than any ideal shepherdess, and are far from being ideal beauties: they are only "meanely fair" in appearance, though graceful; their hair is not very blond, their eyes black. They spend some time chasing sheep out of someone's field of flax, and taking goats to the river to drink. Don Felis' servant Fabio comes from the impoverished "hidalgo" stock of the Cachupines of Laredo, who were notorious for their vanity and conceit. He advises the young page Valerio (Felismena) on how to court a canon's maid, from whom they will thus get abundant supplies of bacon, wine, and fine handkerchiefs.

Music and clothes held a peculiar fascination for Montemayor— naturally enough in the case of music, where he had a professional interest. It is therefore not surprising that music should figure prominently at all levels of *Diana*. In the pastoral world, it was of course essential to the genre that shepherds should spend their time giving vent to their feelings in song. This may well have been part of its attraction for Montemayor. The shepherd's traditional instruments, the rebeck and the pipes, make their appearance in the very first paragraph of *Diana*, and the sound of music pervades from then on the shepherds' world, as an accompaniment to their songs and as a harmony which blends with, and enhances, that of nature.

But it is in the palace of Felicia and in the urban, courtly setting of Felismena's tale that Montemayor, freed from the constraint of the only two rustic instruments available to shepherds, allows his professional knowledge to range more richly. In Felicia's palace, a trio of nymphs (in a musical competition against the shepherds) play a lute, a harp, and a psaltery. Don Felis' serenade to Celia in Book II is minutely described as regards the succession of items and the musical settings, giving us a vivid idea of the kind of concert in which Montemayor himself was a regular performer. The instruments mentioned include cornets, viols, flageolet, sackbut, harp, and virginal.

As for clothes, Montemayor describes them with evident delight. The pastoral world does not offer much opportunity to do so. There, clothes are simple and choice extremely limited: a coarse woolen coat (the traditional *sayal*) for the men, and a skirt and bodice (*saya* and *jubón*) for the women. Even here, though, the charming picture of Belisa, lying asleep when the company of nymphs and shepherds first come upon her, includes a careful indication that she was wearing a pale blue skirt, with a blouse of the same color and a bodice of extremely fine material. When dealing with ladies and courtiers, on the other hand, Montemayor can indulge his taste, knowing that a display of sumptuousness could not fail to interest and please his readers (who either moved in court circles, or wished that they did). The description of Felismena's clothes and jewels when, at Felicia's bidding, she is attired as befits her rank and station in life, is remarkable for its richness and careful detail, based undoubtedly on ladies' fashions at the courts where the author had served. The description of the clothes worn by Don Felis (and of the new blue, white, and gold livery he had adopted for his retinue in homage to Celia) is a riot of color, gorgeous stuffs, pearls, and gold. Felicia's nymphs offer further opportunities of this kind: they wear tunics of finest white cloth embroidered in gold and silver, and are decked in gold, diamonds, and strings of pearls.

VI *The Language: Prose and Poetry*

The combination of prose and poetry offered excellent opportunities for introducing variety into the story while displaying the author's range of literary and metrical skills. It also reflected at the formal level the blend of narrative and lyrical substance that Montemayor was endeavoring to achieve. Not that the prose sections are simply reserved for narrative purposes, while poetry takes care of lyrical effusions. The blend is much more subtle than that. Sometimes the poetry is used to convey narrative information (e.g., when Dórida the nymph describes Sireno's and Diana's parting). Much more pervasively, and in accordance with the general tenor of the novel, much of the prose is informed by a reflective, lyrical attitude. Whether in prose or in poetry, Montemayor's language has been praised for its linguistic purity, remarkable in a writer who was born and grew up in Portugal.[23]

Prose. The prose narrative and descriptive sections flow slowly, in broad, balanced periods. There is an evident concern for balance and symmetry: at the level of vocabulary, each noun is usually accompanied by its characteristic adjective forming thus a basic unit which, with the equipoise of its two components, strikes a leisurely rather than a dynamic note, both in terms of sound and of sense. The perennial, unchanging nature of the ideal pastoral world is suggested by such techniques as the characteristic substantival use of the infinitive. So in this passage, where the sudden shift from the imperfect past to the infinitive lifts Sireno's lament from the consideration of a finite situation to that of an intemporal world (italics added): "¿Viste los favores que me hazía? ¿Viste la blandura de palabra con que me *manifestava* sus amores? ¿Viste cómo *llevar* el ganado al río, *sacar* los corderos al soto, *traer* las ovejas por la siesta a la sombra destos alisos, jamás sin mi compañía supo hazello?" ("Did you see how she favored me? Did you see with what sweet words she manifested her love? Did you see how to lead her flocks to the river, to take her lambs to the grove, to drive her sheep to the shade of these alders, were all tasks she never could perform without my company?") Verbs and clauses are regularly balanced against each other in symmetrical pairs, or arranged in sequences that combine like the phrases of a musical composition. The pursuit of a musical effect is clearly deliberate—and hardly surprising in an author who was a musician by profession.

The characters, too, in soliloquies or in extended recitals of their tribulations, voice their feelings in the same kind of musically flowing language, but variations of tone—repeated exclamations, rhetorical questions, the intensive use of copulative conjunctions (the technique known as *polysyndeton* in classical rhetoric) or, on the contrary, their elimination to convey the rush of emotion (*asyndeton*)— these and other devices are used to heighten the expression of the lovers' states of mind.[24] Dialogue, on the other hand, is handled swiftly and economically, and conducted in language suited to the characters and the occasion. A more dramatic handling of language is also evident in some of the scenes located in the natural, as distinct from the ideal pastoral, world. At all levels, Montemayor's prose reveals a thorough mastery of rhythm and tempo, skillfully varied to suit the writer's purposes.

Poetry. Although Montemayor professed becoming modesty about his own poetic gifts, there is little doubt, on the evidence of his copious *Cancionero*, that in his writing he thought of himself primarily as a poet. And in his one and only prose work, *Diana*, he made a point of displaying the full range of poetic forms and meters in current use at the time. In keeping with his own cultural position (also, to varying degrees, that of his contemporaries in sixteenth-century Spain: well-rooted in the past of medieval thought and forms, but keenly alive to the new humanism from Italy in philosophy and literature), he used with equal enthusiasm both the traditional Spanish *arte menor* forms which form the bulk of fifteenth-century *Cancioneros*, and the hendecasyllabic verse-forms recently brought from Italy to Spain.[25]

Of the three most ambitious poems in *Diana*, two are in Italianate forms (*Canto de Orpheo* and "Si lágrimas no pueden ablandarte") and one in octosyllabic verse (*Canto de la Nimpha*). *Orpheus' Song*, a poem in forty-three *octavas reales*, eulogizes a large number of contemporary Spanish ladies (beginning with Montemayor's two royal patronesses).[26] This is a major stumbling block to the modern reader's enjoyment of *Diana*. The verse is pedestrian, and the praise stereotyped. But the author's contemporaries no doubt enjoyed this feminine *Who's Who*: it was never cut out in subsequent editions (a fate from which unenjoyable portions of works of literature were not immune, as we shall see later in considering the ending of Gil Polo's *Diana enamorada*), and four additional ladies were inserted in the Milan edition of *Diana* (undated, possibly 1560), three of them Italian for greater topicality.

"Si lágrimas no pueden ablandarte" ("If tears cannot cause you to relent"), sung by Silvano and Sireno at the end of Book VI is, on the

other hand, one of the more pleasing compositions in the novel. It is
cast in the mold of the traditionally pastoral amoebaean song (where
two shepherds sing, in alternate stanzas, of their respective loves),
and three different kinds of Italianate verse are skillfully combined in
its four sections. Here Montemayor strikes a note that is at times
strongly reminiscent of Garcilaso. The nymph's song "Junto a una
verde ribera" ("Near to a green river bank"), describing Sireno's and
Diana's original parting, is also in different sections, alternating two
octosyllabic forms (*quintillas* and *redondillas*). It is a complete little
eclogue in itself, lightweight, and entirely successful on its own
terms. It is also worth noting how skillfully it is used at that point in
the story to allow the reader to witness, in flashback, the lovers'
original relationship, with the added poignancy that Sireno, now
rejected and heartbroken, is present at the recital.

Montemayor's verse has been subjected to varying (and on the
whole, not very complimentary) evaluations, ever since Cervantes
(*Don Quixote* I. 6) decreed that virtually all Italianate verse should be
expunged, though he was willing to keep the *arte menor* verse. By
and large, it is correct to say that Montemayor's claim to literary
distinction must rest on the high quality of his prose, and that his
poetry tends to be pedestrian.

His Italianate verse, melodious in a Garcilasian manner,[27] suffers
from time to time from a certain harshness in the rhythm, curious
perhaps in someone with as fine a musical ear as Montemayor, but not
infrequently found in Spanish sixteenth-century poets wrestling to fit
their native habits of thought and meter to the longer line and subtler
relationships of syllabic count and stress-pattern of the Italian hende-
casyllable. Yet not all his efforts in this medium are failures, or merely
derivative. In addition to "Si lágrimas no pueden ablandarte," a
glance at Silvano's *octavas* "Amador soy, mas nunca fuy amado" ("I
am a lover, but was never loved"), Diana's *canción*, "Ojos que ya no
veys quien os mirava" ("Eyes that see not him who looked on you"), or
Alanio's *octavas*, "No mas, Nympha cruel, ya estás vengada" ("No
more, oh cruel Nymph. You are revenged") should be enough to
confirm that this is the case.

As for his compositions in the *arte menor* of the *Cancioneros*, there
is no doubt that they are technically polished and often felicitous
examples of the genre both metrically and in the characteristic use of
antitheses and conceits. For all his display of Italianate forms, it
seems clear that he was most at home in this type of poetry. Two
particularly successful examples of Montemayor's *arte menor*, and

probably the best two poems in *Diana*, are Sireno's *glosa* "Passados contentamientos" ("Past contentment") and Diana's *romance* "Quando triste yo nací" ("When that I, poor soul, was born").

Montemayor's *Diana* was an instant success, not only with the general public (as attested by the many editions and translations) but also with his fellow writers, who were quick to see the possibilities of the new genre. Here was a basically flexible and open-ended form: a simple, low-key narrative thread allowing for any amount of contrasting episodes and lyrical interludes, invested, moreover, with the reflected prestige of its humanistic Italian origins. In the hands of Montemayor's Spanish successors, it became a comprehensive vehicle which could accommodate, with varying degrees of success, all kinds of elements, courtly as well as pastoral, urban as well as rustic. It could combine the emotional appeal of the sentimental romance with the plot interest of tales of adventure and intrigue, and the delicate flow of lyrical poetry with the intellectual exercise of disquisitions on love, literature, aesthetics, or any other subject desired. Something for everyone, in fact, and informed at the same time with the peculiar evocative power of the Golden Age myth. The sequel announced, although not written, by Montemayor provided a ready-made starting point, of which two writers were to take advantage within the next few years; Alonso Pérez's *Diana* came out in 1563, and Gaspar Gil Polo's early in 1564. The former is a pedestrian piece of work (see Chapter 6). Gil Polo's *Diana enamorada*, on the other hand, is a novel of remarkable quality, and stands as one of the most successful examples of the Spanish pastoral novel.

CHAPTER 3

Gaspar Gil Polo: Primera parte de Diana enamorada. Cinco libros que prosiguen los siete de la Diana de Jorge de Montemayor (*First Part of ENAMORED DIANA. Five books which continue the seven of* Diana *by Jorge de Montemayor*).[1]

I *The Author*

GASPAR Gil Polo (d. 1584/85) was born and spent his life in Valencia. He was a notary, and a distinguished civil servant praised by the King for his "trustworthiness, ability, knowledge and loyalty," as well as for remarkable industry. In 1572 he was appointed to a high post in the royal treasury in Valencia, of which he was granted life tenure in 1579. He died in Barcelona, late in 1584 or very early 1585, while on a treasury mission. He left behind a widow, eight or nine children and "a very small estate." Opinions are divided as to whether he is the same Gil Polo (whose first name is not on record) who taught Greek at Valencia University from 1566 to 1573. This is not inherently improbable. His novel is clearly the work of a cultivated mind, well in touch with the humanistic culture of his time, and contains much evidence of familiarity with the classics. Although he appears to have been a well-known figure in Valencian literary circles (he is mentioned at least twice in contemporary lists of Valencian poets), the "continual business and usual occupations" to which he refers in the introduction to the novel seem to have left him little time for writing. Apart from one or two pieces of occasional verse, *Diana enamorada* is his only work.

II   *The Novel*

In an *Epistle to the Readers* the author presents the novel as purely a work of fiction, discusses its literary characteristics, and explains its purpose: to warn against the "pernicious disease" of love.

Book I: By the alder fountain, Diana, still in love with Sireno, laments his indifference. An unknown shepherdess (Alcida) tries to console her. A debate on the power of love between the two is interrupted by Delio, Diana's husband. Unrestrained as well as jealous, he desires Alcida at once, and hastens after her when she flees at the sound of an approaching man's voice. This is Marcelio, seeking Alcida. *Marcelio's tale:* The scion of a noble Seville family, he had been brought up at the Portuguese court. (Here certain details make the reader who is familiar with Montemayor realize that he is Felismena's twin brother.) He had served with distinction in Portuguese North Africa, and become engaged to Alcida, the governor's daughter. As they were all sailing back to Lisbon for the wedding, the ship had been blown into the Mediterranean by a violent storm. Marcelio, Alcida, and her sister Clenarda, with the ship's pilot and another seaman, had been swept away in a lifeboat, leaving the girls' father, Eugerio, and their brother Polydoro behind on board with the rest of the crew. The storm ended, the seamen had abducted Clenarda, contriving to abandon Marcelio and Alcida on separate islands (Ibiza and Formentera), Alcida being deceived into believing that Marcelio had eloped with her sister. Rescued by a passing ship, Alcida, disguised as a shepherdess and abjuring love, wandered through Italy and back to Spain. Marcelio had been following her traces, so far unavailingly. Diana does not feel free to reveal Alcida's proximity, but invites Marcelio to stay overnight in her village. On the next day they will set out together to seek Felicia's help. On their way to the village, they meet Tauriso and Berardo, two of Diana's rejected suitors.

Book II: (From here on, each Book opens with a brief authorial introduction commenting on the action or drawing a moral.) Next morning, on their way to Felicia, Diana and Marcelio discuss the nature and effects of jealousy. They meet Ismenia (from Selvagia's tale in Montemayor) alone and grieving. *Ismenia's tale:* Montano's marriage to Ismenia had angered his widowed father Fileno (who had wanted her for himself). Fileno then married Felisarda, who promptly pursued her new stepson with adulterous proposals, using the maid Silveria as go-between. Seeking revenge for Montano's refusals, Felisarda with Silveria's help planned to trick Montano into killing his father believing him to be an interloper. A last-minute recognition prevented bloodshed, but Felisarda persuaded Fileno that the attempt was deliberate and encouraged by Ismenia, and that Ismenia was herself committing adultery. Montano, publicly accused of attempted parricide, and believing Ismenia's adultery to be true, fled the village. Ismenia, having learnt from a repentant Silveria how the plot had been engineered, and now looking for her husband, joins Diana and Marcelio on their journey to Felicia. They soon come upon Tauriso and Berardo in the company of a mysterious lady and gentleman. Unseen, they listen from behind the bushes.

Book III: Marcelio recognizes Polydoro and Clenarda in the unknown couple. Joyful reunion and *Polydoro's tale*: The battered ship had reached the coast of Valencia, where they had found Clenarda, rescued by fishermen from her kidnappers. An old fisherman has sent them on to Felicia for help in finding Alcida and Marcelio. Felicia had kept old Eugerio, and sent the two young people out. The reunited company now proceed to Felicia, leaving Tauriso and Berardo behind. On the way, Clenarda praises the beauties of Valencia and repeats the *Song of the River Turia* (which she had heard from the river god himself) in praise of famous Valencians. The travellers are met by Arethea, a nymph of Felicia's, as they approach the palace.

Book IV: Arethea announces that Alcida and Sireno, the two nonlovers, are both with Felicia, and that she seems to be planning for them to marry, since they are so well matched. The reader is warned that this is merely a psychological trick to work on Marcelio's and Diana's feelings. On arrival, Diana, Ismenia, and Marcelio are separated from Polydoro and Clenarda, and taken into the palace. Most of the main characters from Montemayor are gathered at Felicia's (Felis and Felismena, Sylvano and Selvagia, Arsileo and Belisa) and Montano's wanderings also lead him there. During that same evening and the next day—against a background of music, song, and beautiful gardens—all situations are resolved through encounters and explanations arranged by Felicia: both Ismenia and Montano and Alcida and Marcelio are reconciled. There is a joyful reunion of the twins Marcelio and Felismena. And a surprise happy ending for Diana and Sireno: Delio, her husband, is dead of a fatal fever brought about by frustration at Alcida's rejection and jealous fury against Diana. Sireno's old love quickly wells up again, now that Diana is free and eager to reciprocate.

Book V: Final celebrations are arranged by Felicia, including a masque (nymphs hunting a white, gold-antlered stag), a guessing game, Belisa's song in praise of women, and a water joust on the river (between two squadrons of richly outfitted boats). Then follows Felicia's concluding speech to the lovers on the evils of improper, and the merits of virtuous, love. The novel ends announcing a further sequel to deal with other characters' still-unresolved love problems.

III   Structure: The Plot and the Characters

Although *Diana enamorada* has been generally praised for the style of its prose and the charm of its lyrics, its structure as a novel has been criticized more than once. Yet Gil Polo's novel is, in fact, notable for economy of structure and variety of incident, and compares favorably with Montemayor's in this respect. Unlike Montemayor's symmetrical structure, Gil Polo's moves in a straight line: in the first three books, various groups of characters converge on Felicia's palace. Once that has been reached, Book IV is devoted to the solution of their problems by purely psychological, and in no way magical, means and the quest is at an end. Book V simply rounds off the novel with celebrations and points up the moral of the story.

A. Prieto, the literary critic,[2] has made an instructive comparison between the different time reference of essential plot events in Montemayor and in Gil Polo. In the former, everything of importance has already happened before the novel begins and, except for Felismena (the one character whose adventure is entirely nonpastoral), all characters regard their sad situations as final. They do nothing to help themselves, but passively accept the respective solutions as they come. None of the events that happen in the novel (as distinct from past events recounted in the tales) contributes to a further unfolding of plot lines. As *Diana* opens, everything is already set for the final resolution, and it is only this closing of accounts, interwoven with flashbacks, comment, and lyrics, that the novel presents.

Of the three plots in *Diana enamorada* (Diana/Delio/Sireno, Marcelio/Alcida, and Ismenia/Montano), on the other hand, the two main ones undergo real developments. Especially the eponymous heroine's: Delio falls in love with Alcida and abandons Diana; she goes to Felicia's palace, ostensibly to seek news of her erring husband, but in fact to meet Sireno; Delio dies; the knowledge of this event alters Sireno's determination, etc. The Marcelio/Alcida story, though involving substantial flashbacks, is far from played out when the novel begins, with the young man in anguished quest, and there is interaction between these two plots (Delio's infatuation for Alcida and its fatal consequences). The Ismenia/Montano tale is functionally much nearer to the closed kind of inserted tale, but even here Ismenia is seeking her partner, and is not merely a passive sufferer.

In Gil Polo, all characters are, to varying degrees, taking an active hand in the shaping of their own destinies. The gain in terms of narrative interest and immediacy is undeniable. What is more, this active disposition on the part of the characters is the necessary manifestation, at the structural level, of Gil Polo's ideological insistence on free will and moral responsibility: *Diana enamorada* is deliberately constructed to illustrate the author's moral thesis. Perhaps, for all his skill and delicacy, a shade too deliberately. What is gained in terms of simplicity and directness may be lost in depth of suggestive power, since the need to illustrate a thesis inevitably conditions the presentation of the characters. Gil Polo is writing to demonstrate that man's will is free, and that reason can control passion. The resulting stress on a rational explanation of events makes for a degree of realism. But it also lands Gil Polo in the difficulty of having to assume that lovers' emotions are amenable to reason. The same theoretical postulates that impel him away from the ambiguities of Montemayor's world prevent him from giving his characters sufficiently complex motivations. His lovers' hearts are of one piece with their minds: Alcida's abhorrence of Marcelio vanishes, without transition, as soon as she learns she has misjudged him. Sireno's change of heart, too, is instantaneous upon hearing of Delio's death.

This is not to say that Gil Polo does not take much trouble to justify, in psychological terms, the changes brought about under Felicia's guidance. In Book IV, the application of techniques of persuasion and gradual psychological preparation is shown in detail: the pairs of lovers are kept separate until the right psychological moment while their emotions are worked upon by suspense, misunderstandings are cleared, and new information made available. As for Sireno, it is essential to note that, throughout the novel, Gil Polo steadfastly ignores the role of the magic potion in Montemayor, and stresses instead the natural explanation: Diana's rebuffs and marriage had cooled her lover's ardors.[3]

Gil Polo attempts a realistic presentation of character and motivation based, except for the over-optimistic estimate of the power of reason, on a common-sense view of human nature. In so doing, he makes his own contribution toward the nurturing of the mental climate in which the modern novel was to develop. Yet, paradoxically, his more realistic characters can strike the reader as less real than Montemayor's. In the first *Diana*, the lyrical musing and delving into the characters' feelings creates a certain illusion of depth. In *Diana enamorada*, the author's scope is limited by the desire to produce, at the same time as a work of entertainment, a model exemplifying a theory of the essential reasonableness of human behavior.

IV   The Ideas: Theory of Love

The traditional view [4] that Gil Polo was merely content to carry forward the unfinished business from the first *Diana* to a happy ending, with the help of magic arts, is patently untrue as regards the means of Felicia's intervention. As for the views that inform the work, an examination of Gil Polo's love theory shows that *Diana enamorada* must, in fact, be regarded as "a criticism of the first Diana," [5] rather than its sequel in any but a superficial sense. The purpose of the book is emphatically stated in the introductory *Epistle*: to make clear the dangerous power of love and the sufferings it inflicts, and to stress the importance of avoiding this pernicious disease. The point is immediately driven home in Alcida's long opening speech to Diana which unfolds a strongly argued criticism of lovers rather than of love. It is they who, by surrendering to passion, are responsible for their own sufferings. Cupid, the traditional symbol of the power of love, is simply a figment of the imagination, a projection of human weaknesses and desires.[6] The essence of the whole speech with its categorical assertion of free will is summarized in the sonnet quoted by Alcida: "Love is not blind, but I, who fondly guide /My will along the path of amorous pain."

Through its prominent placing and earnest moral tone, this speech is clearly designed to carry the introductory warning into the action proper, and to set the love stories in proper perspective. The development of the various plots, though it is not without occasional reminders, contains little in the way of direct admonition, except for a powerful indictment of jealousy in Book II, to which we shall presently return. After the main action is over, however, readers are again reminded of the moral, this time by Felicia herself. The festivities in Book V include two allegorical performances intended to edify as well as entertain: the stag hunt and the water joust. Felicia explains the stag hunt: the nymphs represent "human inclinations," the white stag is the "human heart" assailed by them. The heart, by exercising its "discretion" (i.e., good judgment) must endeavor to protect itself from their harmful shots, and seek safety in flight when necessary. The water joust allegory is sufficiently obvious not to need elucidation. Of the two opposing squadrons, one is decked in gay colors, white and crimson, the other in mournful mulberry and yellow. The white-and-crimson squadron's victory clearly symbolizes the triumph of joy over sorrow; joy has now replaced sorrow in the lovers' hearts. We shall later see, however, that there is also a further implication. In her final speech to the lovers,[7] Felicia again stresses the didactic purpose of their adventures, and attacks the fatalistic view of the power of love. The sequel to Montemayor's *Diana* is thus a deliberate indictment of the fatalistic love philosophy which had inspired the earlier novel. But Gil Polo is not condemning all human love. Felicia distinguishes between two kinds of love. One is that symbolized by Cupid which, while claiming to be spiritual and chaste, is actually inspired by "wanton craving." The distinguishing characteristic of this kind of love, "which concerns itself with low things," is the suffering it causes. And suffering, since it is the mark of love born of "sensual and greedy craving" is not, as Montemayor would have it, something to be proud of, but precisely the evidence that condemns the wanton lover by revealing the impurity of his love.

Another kind of love, however, which is firmly based on reason leads the mind on to the consideration of higher things. This is "virtuous and permitted love, through which we grow attached to virtues, skills, perfections, wisdom and heavenly things," and it causes no suffering, but brings joy and happiness. The distinction, of which the shepherds and shepherdesses were unaware, is clear: both kinds of love claim to be chaste and spiritual but one, that which causes suffering and is symbolized by Cupid, is nothing of the sort, being rather desire in disguise, and hence to be eschewed. There remains therefore only *one* legitimate kind of love, that which is founded on "true and certain reason" and is a source of contentment. This love is, of course, entirely consistent with the emphasis on free will and individual responsibility which characterizes *Diana enamorada*.

The contrast between "Cupid" and "virtuous and permitted love" is illustrated in the discussion on love, in the traditional form of a song contest, between Sireno and Arsileo in Book IV. At first this seems to be nothing but the usual disputation between the *enamorado* and the *desamorado*, the happy and the disgruntled lover, which is an integral part of the pastoral convention. Read in the light of Felicia's words, however, it reveals itself, more significantly, as a poetic presentation of the nature of the two kinds of love: good love, guided by reason, fits into the life-giving pattern of nature and is a source of joy; evil love destroys all capacity for rational decision and is, in an ultimate sense, unnatural because the suffering it causes is a discord jarring against the harmony of nature. The views of the two shepherds are therefore not contradictory but complementary, and the argument a device for presenting Gil Polo's philosophy of love in poetic form. The water joust allegory, too, now reveals its full significance. The triumph of joy over sorrow in the lovers' hearts is not just the natural effect of a happy outcome, but a symbol of the triumph of good over evil love, since joy and contentment can only flow, by definition, from the good love.

This stress on the joyfulness of true love, an attitude which informs the whole of *Diana enamorada*, is one of the most remarkable aspects of the book, and contrasts strikingly with the sorrowing quality characteristic of Montemayor's *Diana* and generally ascribed (not always rightly) to sixteenth-century pastoral as a whole. The picture is completed, and the message driven home, by showing the disastrous effects of evil love: Delio, the one character in the book who comes to an unpleasant end, stands as an awful example of what surrender to the passions and, in particular, jealousy can do to a man. On this subject, too, illustration through character and incident is reinforced by a theoretical statement: the debate concerning jealousy in Book II. Once again Diana maintains the standard view, namely that jealousy is a "manifest token of love" and inseparable from it. This Marcelio utterly rejects arguing that, although few lovers may entirely escape jealousy, yet the "more perfect and truer lover" is he who is exempt from that passion, proving thereby the "worth, power and purity of his desire." This he expands with an eloquent picture of the evils resulting from jealousy, which is compared at length to a disease. Jealous love causes the most intense and hopeless suffering; but suffering is the mark of evil love. It follows therefore that jealousy is incompatible with the good love, and Marcelio's rejection of the traditional position is the necessary consequence of the distinction on which the whole book's argument rests. Jealousy, far from being the pride of true love, is the shame of the evil one.

Delio's jealousy reveals the tainted quality of his feelings: he has abdicated responsibility, and surrendered to evil love. It is therefore natural that he should also furnish the one outstanding example of unbridled desire in his irresponsible pursuit of Alcida. Throughout the novel, he is the only character that remains a prey to uncontrolled passions, and they kill him in the end. His death is, quite literally, his own fault. The contrast between him and Marcelio, the reasonable, ever-constant lover, could not be more pointed, and it is peculiarly fitting that the former's jealousy should be condemned out of the latter's mouth.

In this connection, it is worth noting that, apart from Felicia's summing up, it is Alcida and Marcelio, the aristocratic lovers portrayed throughout the book as models of constant and correct behavior, who expound the true interpretation of love in the two major speeches (Alcida's on love and free will and Marcelio's on jealousy). In both instances, their words are addressed to Diana who undergoes a process of sentimental reeducation through the example and precept of the paragon lovers and under the guidance of Felicia, whose final speech relates the now-complete design to the didactic aims stated in the introduction. The whole novel is thus a sort of miniature *Bildungsroman* in which Diana (and, with her, the other shepherds and shepherdesses) develops from the confusion attendant upon any degree of evil love to the joy and happiness of good love.

It has been argued that the paramount position of reason in Gil Polo's theory reveals a strong element of Stoicism.[8] While it is true that right reason, seen as an all-pervading divine fire, is the cornerstone of Stoic philosophy, it is essential to bear in mind that there was, in the sphere of ethics, a very long history of mutual interaction between Stoicism and Neoplatonism.[9] As was seen in chapter 1, an insistence on the necessary, positive connection between love and reason was, in fact, very much part of the mainstream of Renaissance Neoplatonism, and Gil Polo was first and foremost a Neoplatonist [10] though, it may be agreed, with a heightened Stoic coloring. In his ideological criticism of Montemayor, he countered his predecessor's views by adopting, in effect, a more purely Neoplatonic viewpoint.

But, at a certain point, Gil Polo's position parts company from Neoplatonism as well. The pure Neoplatonic relationship between lovers, being only an early step on the ladder leading to divine love, is ultimately transcended. First the senses, then the beloved herself, are left behind on the way to God. Gil Polo's chaste love, on the other hand, displays a robust measure of common sense: it does not seek to go beyond the human sphere, but finds fulfillment which includes both body and soul in marriage: "the union" (in Casella's words) "of two free wills in the creation of a shared joy." [11]

V *Literary Form and Technique: Narrative and Description; Realism and Verisimilitude; The Author's Presence*

Although he was illustrating a theoretical point, Gil Polo was very much aware of the need to hold the reader's interest in plot, character, and incident. His skill in combining plot elements effectively at the entertainment level, while at the same time furthering his didactic purpose, is well exemplified in the initial scene between Diana and Alcida, which subtly serves a dual purpose: the heroine inherited from Montemayor is at once brought into contact with a character created by Gil Polo in a smooth transition that both harks back to the first novel, and points forward to the new one. At the same time, Alcida's new way of looking at things, contrasting with Diana's sorrowful recall of past events, marks the beginning of the shepherdess's sentimental reeducation.

For exciting narrative materials, Gil Polo turned to the Greek romances. Both Marcelio's and Polydoro's complementary tales can aptly be described as being "miniature examples of the most characteristic features of Greek Byzantine stories: travels, storms, abductions, forced separations, recognitions," [12] and Ismenia's tale is a straight borrowing from Heliodorus' *Ethiopian Story*. [13] The world of action and adventure plays an essential role in *Diana enamorada*; the trains of adventurous events, the flights and pursuits, heartbreaks and misunderstandings started in North Africa, at sea, and elsewhere, flow together in the pastoral setting of the first three books, and are brought to a conclusion in Felicia's courtly pleasure gardens in Books IV and V. In keeping with the character of the narrative, descriptions of dynamic sequences of events predominate over those of static settings. Obvious examples are the set-piece of storm description in Marcelio's tale and the swift succession of events when the brigand sailors overpower Marcelio and sail away with him and Clenarda, while Alcida signals desperately from the shore; or, in Ismenia's story, the description of Montano's night attack on his father; and the fishermen's description of Clenarda's rescue in Polydoro's tale.

Some of the action carries over into the pastoral world, as in the account of Alcida's hasty flight from Marcelio into the forest or the scene of the reunion of Marcelio with Polydoro and Clenarda. And even in Felicia's gardens, descriptions of things that happen—such as the stag hunt and (with much lively detail) the water joust—take pride of place over those of things that simply are. This is not to say that Gil Polo is unaware of what he owes to the pastoral tradition by way of placing his characters in suitable natural surroundings. He was familiar with the classics, he knew his Sannazaro, and he was a gifted enough writer. He had thus no difficulty in producing the pleasing, harmonious natural settings proper to the pastoral world. Yet the pastoral setting is less central to Gil Polo than it was to Montemayor. For all its abstraction and generality, nature in the first *Diana* was steeped in the splendor of the Platonic world of Ideas, and its radiant presence was constantly interwoven with the texture of the novel. Gil Polo's natural settings, on the other hand, are sketched in at infrequent intervals, strictly according to the requirements of the story.

In the last two Books of *Diana enamorada*, the story leaves the pastoral world altogether, and moves within the confines of Felicia's gardens. Here, too, comparison with Montemayor shows both a change in the status of the setting and a lesser degree of involvement with it. The supernatural world of Montemayor's Felicia, described in abundant realistic detail, but utterly fantastic, has become the pleasure gardens of a certainly wise, but in no way magical lady, where problems are solved by rational means, and richly attired ladies and gentlemen, joined by hardly less sophisticated shepherds and shepherdesses, engage in courtly guessing-games, songs, dances, and other revelries. The amount of description is minimal. Deliberately so, for, as Gil Polo says, he need not take time to expatiate on the beauties and riches of the palace and the gardens, since it was all declared at length in the first *Diana*.

The references back to Montemayor, in addition to doing away with the need for lengthy descriptions, serve also to underline the connection between the second and the first *Diana*, which Gil Polo was at pains to keep before the reader. For instance, the phrase signaling the first glimpse of Felicia's palace in *Diana enamorada* is taken straight from Montemayor's more elaborate description. Where Montemayor had written about "a great dwelling composed of such high and superb buildings that they gave great pleasure to the beholders, because the *spires which reared above the trees* gave forth such great radiance that they seemed made of the finest crystal," Gil Polo simply states that "they saw that they were very close to Diana's temple, and began to distinguish its tall *spires which reared above the*

trees" (italics added).[14] Gil Polo characteristically omits reference to
the crystal-like radiance of the superb buildings, and fastens on to the
bare fact of the tall spires, a difference which tellingly sums up the
contrast in the atmosphere surrounding Felicia in the two writers.
    Gil Polo's descriptions of characters are equally spare. The beauty
of both shepherdesses and ladies must, of course, be taken for
granted. So much so, that on Diana's first appearance even the
customary bare reference to the fact is omitted. This comes later—
only once—and one mention of her delicate voice and charming
delivery of a song and another of her white hand and golden hair, are
all we find about Diana's beauty in the narrative passages of the book.
Only in Tauriso's and Berardo's songs do we find a few more intima-
tions (hardly to be avoided there since the songs are about her), but
even then in the most general terms, (eyes like stars, golden hair,
etc.). And this is far more than any other feminine character in the
novel is given. Alcida's "most extreme beauty" does rate a little praise
in Marcelio's first verse-letter to her, but her sister Clenarda's
charms, powerfully though they turned the sailor's brain, are taken
entirely on trust. Ismenia's voice is mellow, and Montano once
compares her eyes in the most common of similes to two suns. The
nymphs' golden locks receive two mentions. Apart from a very few
other scattered references (such as the "fine and rare marble" of a
shepherdess' skin), this is the sum total of Gil Polo's efforts to portray
the beauty or, for that matter, the appearance of his characters.
Clothes are given equally short shrift, as witness Marcelio and Alcida
putting on the clothes proper to their rank and station: Marcelio's
clothes are simply "so rich and embellished with gold and precious
stones that they were of infinite value" and Alcida, even more sparingly, dresses "richly with the clothes and jewels which [Felicia] had
ordered should be given to her."
    Such treatment may seem perfunctory, but is entirely consistent
with Gil Polo's approach and interests. On the evidence of *Diana
enamorada*, his imagination was not of a sensuously vivid kind and,
unlike the lyrical and gently sensuous Montemayor, he was interested in the clash and interplay of minds and events rather than in
mood and description. So, he wisely took advantage of the established conventions of the tradition in which he was writing. Readers
of pastoral would automatically assume that meadows were green,
waters murmurous, and shepherdesses beautiful and golden-haired,
and the author need do no more than supply the briefest of remind-

ers. The two passages where description is lively and detailed, the stag hunt and the water joust, are, significantly enough, those that illustrate the moral of the story.[15]

Sparing though Gil Polo may be of circumstantial details, those he does supply are put to purposeful, realistic use as a means of anchoring his stories and their characters to the real world of reason and responsibility. As has been seen, specific geographical references abound in Marcelio's and Polydoro's tales of adventure, while the exact location of the pastoral lands and Felicia's pleasure gardens in the real world, although not explicitly stated, is implicitly identified by reference back to Montemayor. Realistic touches here and there heighten the sense of adventure: Marcelio's and Alcida's ship, sailing from Ceuta to Lisbon, is swept far into the Mediterranean by a westerly gale whose force is increased by the funnelling constriction of the Straits of Gibraltar: a violent blast from starboard almost sinks her, and another from port flings the lifeboat from the ship.

Nor is the human frame's need for food and rest disregarded, either in the world of adventure or in that of pastoral. Resting in the shade during the midday heat while consuming a rustic meal had, of course, been part and parcel of the pastoral tradition ever since Theocritus. But additional touches such as specifying that Marcelio had had no food or rest all day, or showing Diana, in spite of her eagerness to set out in the early morning, stopping not only to pick up her rustic flute, but also to fill her bag with victuals are Gil Polo's own. As for references to the importance of avoiding exertion in the heat of day, they are plentiful enough to make one wonder to what extent Gil Polo himself may have suffered from the heat of Valencian summers.[16] Beyond such little touches of realism (which are not uncommon in the genre), what is peculiar to Gil Polo is his overall concern with consistency and credibility. This is primarily apparent in the handling of the characters' psychology and in the emphasis on the natural means used to bring about the final solutions. It also emerges in other connections, for instance, the need felt from time to time to justify the unlikely degree of artistry displayed by the shepherds or, alternatively, to claim that their native simplicity is more satisfying than courtly sophistication. Another case in point is the stress on their status as true shepherds, unused to pomp and luxury, as well as the scrupulous observance of strict propriety important to someone with Gil Polo's ethical concerns.[17] One should, however, refrain from reading into these and similar details a pursuit of "realism" in the nineteenth-century sense of the term. The concern for verisimilitude is a specifically literary requirement resulting from the application of current Aristotelian theory, and is consistent with Gil Polo's character (as it emerges throughout) as a thoughtful man of letters with a solid cultural background, setting out to compose a carefully wrought piece of literature according to the best canons of the time.

Sannazaro portrayed himself in *Arcadia* in the character of Sincero. Sireno, in the first *Diana*, may or may not have been intended to represent Montemayor. In *Diana enamorada*, where all the characters are explicitly fictitious, the author's presence in the work is more distant, yet more explicitly asserted. Instead of using one of the characters as a mask, the author is openly present, in his own person, to comment and reflect on the tale he is telling. He is so, normally enough, in the introductory *Epistle to Readers*. But he also reappears at regular intervals during the action, especially in the authorial comments which introduce Books II, III, IV, and V, a sort of minuscule additional *Epistles* covering standard topics such as the cruelty of so-called Love, the fickleness of Fortune, and the fury of a woman scorned (Books II and III). He appears again in more individual and refreshingly commonsensical remarks, such as the dry comment that men call Fortune fickle when it works against them, but happily accept its favors, when they come, as a matter of course (Book IV). He also makes a point from time to time of reminding the reader that the story is under direct authorial control by inserting a brief first-person clause (e.g., "Around this fountain, *as I said*, they all sat down.") This technique not only stresses the fictional and, in Gil Polo's case, cautionary nature of the tale, but it also establishes a closer, almost confidential, relationship between author and reader. The dual perspective (the characters as they see themselves and as seen by the author) opens up a range of possibilities for operating at various levels. Embryonic in Gil Polo, this approach was to yield rich fruit in the multiple perspectives and subtle complexities of Cervantes' *Don Quixote*.

VI *The Language: Prose and Poetry*

Menéndez Pelayo, the pioneer critic, defined Gil Polo's prose as "highly cultivated, delightful and polished," and praised its "elegance and classical quality," while claiming it showed occasional "small blemishes" in the form of traces of Valencian and Italian linguistic influences.[18] Further analysis, however, has shown little that can unequivocally be attributed to the influence of Gil Polo's native Valencian. As for the Italianisms, most of them were already in use prior to *Diana enamorada*, and had become, or were in the process of becoming, common literary currency in sixteenth-century Castilian. The same can be said of the abundance of *cultismos* (learned terms). On the other hand, Gil Polo has a characteristic manner of resorting at times to words and constructions that were by then somewhat obsolete and carried an archaic medieval flavor.[19]

It has been suggested that the blending of Valencian, Italian, archaic, and colloquial elements was part of a deliberate effort to achieve "a specific type of pastoral prose" on the pattern of Sannazaro's, and that Gil Polo was, "in Spain, the most brilliant prose writer in the style of [Sannazaro's] *Arcadia*." [20] He was at any rate a prose writer who fashioned a highly efficient instrument for himself. He was perfectly at ease in the more solemn, high-sounding style, complete with rhetorical devices and latinizing constructions, that had characterized the vogue of sentimental novels and romances of chivalry. He uses it in the opening pages of the novel, as if to mark its beginning in a suitably impressive manner, and returns briefly to it when occasion and literary propriety demand; for instance, in the purposely "literary" description of a fountain and its surroundings in Book III, directly imitated from Sannazaro's *Arcadia* and formally introduced by an explicit reference to the Italian author. But as soon as the literary embellishment is over, the prose flows again in short, unforced, natural periods. The most characteristic feature of Gil Polo's prose style is its unobtrusiveness. He endeavored to produce what was, in the context of his time, a remarkably plain and flexible medium which moved the story forward while fitting itself pleasingly, excitingly, or argumentatively, as required, to its up and downs, but without drawing attention to itself.

His poetry, on the other hand, is designed as a deliberate display of skill and technique, to which he draws the reader's attention in the introductory *Epistle* by pointing to the "variety of verses and subjects" and claiming the introduction of new forms ("so far, to my knowledge, not used in this language") modeled on old Provençal and French poetry. Apart from these few forms, his range of versification is very similar to that of Montemayor, and represents the mixture of traditional and Italianate meters that was fast becoming typical of Spanish pastoral novels.[21] Traditional meters are not Gil Polo's main focus of interest, although he handles them with impeccable skill, and an evident delight in experimenting. He uses them mostly for slight occasional pieces, although there are a few more ambitious compositions—for instance, Diana's *coplas reales* "Mi sufrimiento cansado" ("My weary sorrow"), with which the novel opens, and Sireno's *quintillas* "Goze el amador contento" ("Let the favored lover enjoy"), the *Canto de Florisia* in defense of women (Book V), and the *Canción de Nerea* (Book III), both in *quintillas*. The latter is a variation on the classical theme of Polyphemus and Galatea, handled with delightful freshness. Although the meter is traditional, the subject and manner reflect the sensibility of the Italian Renaissance. Unlike Montemayor, Gil Polo was entirely a man of the new age, and adapted the old forms to the new flow of language and imagery. It is natural, therefore, that Italianate verse should be prominent: thirteen sonnets, five *canciones*, many *octavas reales* and *tercetos* (both alone and combined with other forms), and one *sextina* are the main bearers of lyrical mood and reflective statement. Here, too, Gil Polo is formally at his most ambitious, experimenting with different types of verses, rhymes, and stanzas to build up ambitious and complex structures, as in Tauriso's and Berardo's amoebaean song "Pues ya se esconde el sol tras las montañas" ("As the sun now goes down behind the hills," Book I), where he combines *octavas* with end-of-line rhyme, *octavas* with internal rhyme (the Italian *rim'almezzo*), and a *canción*.

The "Provençal Rhymes" and "French Verses" are further examples of Gil Polo's interest in prosodic experiment. The two "Provençal" compositions employ a twelve-line stanza combining hendecasyllables with pentasyllables, which seems to be of his own invention, since no specific Provençal model has been found. The rhyme-pattern is similar to that used by Garcilaso in his Eclogue I. This is suggestive, in view of the fact that the first "Provençal" composition has definite echoes, and even one direct textual quotation, from that eclogue. Whatever their formal inspiration, in these compositions Gil Polo showed that a very harmonious stanza of considerable rhythmic pliancy could be achieved by means of an unusual combination which, however, found little favor with later authors.

The one composition in "French" verse is given pride of place at the end of Book IV, being the epithalamium celebrating Sireno's and Diana's marriage. Its nine-verse stanzas are built up of combined fourteen and seven-syllable lines. As the long line has a regular caesura after the seventh syllable, the alternation is, in effect, between full and half lines. The basic long line made up of two seven-syllable hemistichs is very much a native of Spain: the Spanish alexandrine of medieval epic and hagiographic poems. But where this plodded sturdily rather than moving gracefully, Gil Polo's varied patterning gives it a stately, melodious flow which may well have been inspired by the French alexandrine stanzas of his contemporary, Pierre de Ronsard.

One piece of versification, not poetry, the modern reader must leave aside unless reading for purposes of historical study—the *Canto de Turia* in praise of eminent Valencians. It is forty-four *octavas reales* long and thoroughly stereotyped. In this respect, as in so many others, Montemayor's *Diana* had set the tone for subsequent authors, and no pastoral novel was felt to be complete without a long laudatory poem. Montemayor had praised beautiful ladies; Gil Polo and others took as their objects men distinguished in letters or other fields. It was a convenient way of generating good will by fitting in actual or possible patrons, and friends or fellow writers of whom one approved (or, equally significantly perhaps, leaving out those whom one disliked). Even this brief discussion suffices to make it clear that Gil Polo's interest in form and technique was considerable, and well-informed, although this offers, of course, no assurance that he was a writer of good poetry. Fortunately, his knowledge and enthusiasm were matched by taste, skill, and genuine, though not very profound, poetic gifts. The result was poetry of a quality that has earned him praise even from those who tend to the wholesale condemnation of pastoral novels.

VII *Literary Sources*

It has been noted that Gil Polo's writing in poetry and prose is the product of a well-stocked mind, making discriminating use of literary allusion, reference, and imitation. His range is wide: Montemayor and Sannazaro; the ever-present background of the Latin classics, Virgil especially, but also Horace, Ovid, and Catullus; the Greek romances for plots and adventures; Bembo and Castiglione for the underlying philosophy of love; Garcilaso, preeminent as a poetic influence, and Petrarch. To a lesser but discernible extent, Dante, Ariosto, Gil Vicente, and others (such as Straparolo, Ariosto's younger contemporary) also provided models. Although *Diana enamorada* cannot be described, as the Italian *Arcadia* has been, as a mosaic of materials and reminiscences, it is certainly closer in this respect to Sannazaro's novel than to Montemayor's. This is not the place to analyze Gil Polo's sources in detail—a field in which, in spite of some good studies,[22] much remains to be done—but attention may be drawn to the importance of two classical themes, and to that of Garcilaso and Petrarch, both as direct sources in themselves and as transmitters of the classical tradition. The classical themes are the praise of country life in imitation of Horace's Epode II: *Beatus ille*, and the tale of Polyphemus and Galatea from Ovid's *Metamorphoses*, both of which were imitated time and again by bucolic poets, to the extent of becoming inextricably involved with the pastoral tradition. The Ovidian tale is brought in twice by Gil Polo: together with Virgil's Ninth Eclogue, it supplies the theme for the *Canción de Nerea* (itself modeled on the second of Sannazaro's Latin piscatory eclogues); also, at one point in Book III, Berardo's praise of Diana's beauty, inspired directly by Garcilaso's Third Eclogue, derives ultimately from Polyphemus' praise of Galatea in the *Metamorphoses*. As for the *Beatus ille*, Gil Polo, familiar as he was with Garcilaso's masterly version in his Second Eclogue, produces his own pleasingly musical rendering of the topic in the last four stanzas of the "Provençal Rhymes" in Book I. Intent upon putting his materials to novel creative use, he introduces a formal variation by having it sung in alternate stanzas by Diana and Alcida, in a sort of feminine version of the typically pastoral amoebaean song. In connection with the Latin classics, it is also worth noting that Gil Polo introduced the epithalamium into Spanish poetry. The "French verses" at the end of Book IV are the first example of the nuptial genre brought to a high pitch of perfection by Catullus and show—in structure, prosody, and tone—a combination of elements that seems to indicate close familiarity with the Latin poet.[23]

Petrarch and Garcilaso are present at many points. Petrarch, whose influence had pervaded European lyric poetry for three centuries and more, came to Gil Polo through all of his immediate sources. A good example of this is the *canzona* "Chiare, fresche e dolci acque," ("Clear waters, fresh and sweet") imitations of which Gil Polo would have found in Sannazaro and, no less than three times, in Garcilaso, as well as in Boscán. As for Garcilaso, like every poet of his generation (and throughout the sixteenth century), Gil Polo had grown up under his spell. Polo's own Neoplatonism and his interest as a poet in the new Italian forms and meters of which Garcilaso had been the undisputed master could only enhance the affinity. He was steeped in Garcilaso's poetry, and his own Italianate verse bears abundant witness to a sensibility thoroughly informed by that of the great model. He displays to a very high degree Garcilaso's characteristic qualities of simplicity, musicality, and elegance. In imagery, vocabulary, and prosody, the echoes and similarities are manifold, whole verses being sometimes quoted in deliberate homage to the master.[24]

In his only work of literature, Gil Polo created one of the most attractive of pastoral novels, in which narrative and lyrical elements are successfully integrated into a lively and harmonious whole. Its quality was recognized at once (Cervantes declaring [*Don Quixote*, Part I, Ch. 6], with a pun on the author's name, that it should be preserved "as if it were by Apollo himself") and it continued to earn critical praise even while the reputation of the genre was at its lowest ebb in later times. More recently, in the new climate of a better understanding of pastoral, it has even been described as "one of the most beautiful Spanish works of the sixteenth century, in both its prose and its verse." [25]

Together with Montemayor's *Diana* (and leaving aside for the moment Alonso Pérez's pedestrian effort—see Chapter 6), it forms the diptych which started the great vogue of Spanish pastoral novels. Ideologically, it stands, as we have seen, in deliberate contrast to its predecessor. In this respect it exemplifies the new sense of ethical commitment which was becoming increasingly apparent in Spanish literature but which flowed thereafter in other literary channels, especially the picaresque novel. The pastoral genre continued primarily as a form of entertainment literature unmarked, on the whole, by any great degree of earnestness. In the hands of two of the greatest writers of the age it did, however, bring forth two works of broader scope and richer connotations: Cervantes' *Galatea* and Lope de Vega's *Arcadia*.

CHAPTER 4

Miguel de Cervantes Saavedra: Primera Parte de Galatea Dividida en Seis Libros (*First Part of* Galatea *Divided in Six Books*)[1]

I *The Author*

NO introduction is needed for the most famous author in Spanish literature, but it may be convenient to recapitulate a few facts. Miguel de Cervantes Saavedra (1547-1616) was born in Alcalá de Henares, the son of impoverished gentlefolk. In 1569 he was in Italy, first in the service of Cardinal Acquaviva, then enlisted in the Spanish army. In 1571 he fought at Lepanto, and was maimed in his left hand. In 1575, sailing back to Spain after leaving the army, he was captured by Turkish pirates, and spent five years at Algiers before being ransomed. On his return to Spain at the age of thirty-three he had been away for twelve adventurous and highly formative years; he had known the culture and charm of Italy, the buffeting of storms, the dangers of war, and the trials of captivity. All this was to supply much material for his literary works. Married in 1584, he could not live by his pen and from 1587 was a minor government agent travelling, mostly in southern Spain, to purchase stores and supplies. He was in Valladolid in 1604, and in 1606 followed the Court to Madrid, where he died in 1616. *Galatea* (1585) was his first published work, and represents, together with some plays, an initial unsuccessful bid to establish himself as a writer. It was only twenty years later that the immense success of *Don Quixote*, Part I (1605), made his reputation. There followed the *Exemplary Novels* (1613), *Eight Plays and Eight*

New Interludes, and *Don Quixote*, Part II (1615). The novel *Persiles and Sigismunda* appeared posthumously (1617).

II   *The Novel*[2]

An "Introduction To Curious Readers" defends the writing of pastoral and the literary dignity of the Spanish language. *Book I*: On the banks of the Tagus, Galatea's suitors Elicio and Erastro see one stranger killing another. Later, Elicio learns the killer's story. *Lisandro's tale*: In Andalusia, Lisandro's and Leónida's love was thwarted by the feud between their families. Their elopement had been tragically foiled by grudge-bearing Carino, who had tricked Leónida's violent brother Crisalvo into murdering her, mistaking her for another. Lisandro had at once killed Crisalvo in revenge (disabling him and then stabbing him with the dagger held in Leónida's dead hand). Since then he had been pursuing Carino, to wreak upon him the vengeance just witnessed by the shepherds. Next morning, Galatea and Florisa (after a brief encounter with Elicio, Erastro, and Lisandro) meet Teolinda, in distress. *Teolinda's tale, part I*: A farmer's daughter from a village on the banks of the Henares, she had fallen in love with Artidoro, a handsome stranger, during a village festival. The tale is interrupted by Aurelio, Galatea's father, and some shepherds pursuing a hare (saved by Galatea's intervention). There follows a picnic on the grass, a debate on love (Elicio and Erastro argue against Lenio, contemptuous of love and lovers), and the return to the village at dusk. Lisandro departs and is never heard of again. *Book II*: *Teolinda's tale, part II*: Teolinda's sister Leonarda—as like her as if they were identical twins—had maliciously deceived Artidoro into believing Teolinda no longer loved him. He had rushed away, hinting at suicide. Teolinda was now anxiously seeking him on the banks of his native Tagus. Next morning, Tirsi and Damón, two "famous shepherds" from Alcalá and Madrid, arrive to attend the wedding of Galatea's fellow villagers Daranio and Silveria. With Elicio and Erastro, they visit a mysterious young man who has been doing penance in a hermitage, take him to the village, and hear his story. *Silerio's tale, part I*: Timbrio and Silerio, two gentlemen of Jerez, in Andalusia, were the closest of friends. When Timbrio went to Naples (to escape the wrath of a powerful enemy while a formal duel on neutral ground was being arranged), Silerio had followed him, and saved his life by risking his own when he was about to be executed (having been mistaken for a bandit leader) in a Catalan coastal town. In the confusion caused by a night attack on the town by Turkish pirates, both friends had managed to escape. In Naples, Silerio had selflessly helped Timbrio woo Nísida, the daughter of noble Spanish parents, although he loved her himself, a fact which he kept hidden by feigning an interest in her sister Blanca (who was herself nursing an unavowed passion for him). The tale is interrupted by the arrival of Daranio and others.

Book III: Silerio's tale, part II: On the day of Timbrio's duel, Silerio's mistake in not wearing the sign of Timbrio's victory (a white scarf tied to his arm) when hastening back to Nísida with the news caused her to believe her lover killed. She fainted and was thought to be dead. Timbrio rushed away in suicidal despair. As soon as she recovered, Nísida set out to look for him, accompanied by her sister; Silerio had retired to a hermitage. Daranio's and Silveria's wedding takes place the next day. Events include: a discussion on love between Elicio and Erastro; Lenio "the loveless" sings an ironical epithalamium; wedding and banquet; performance of a verse eclogue (by Orompo, Orfenio, Crisio, and Masilio) illustrating four different kinds of love suffering: death of the beloved, jealousy, absence, unrequited love; Damón's discourse on the evils of jealousy; poetic contest between "free" (i.e., unattached) Lauso and another shepherd; rustic epithalamium by old Arsindo.

Book IV: Next morning, Galatea, Florisa, and Teolinda witness Rosaura successfully extort a promise of marriage from Grisaldo by attempting to stab herself in his presence. Rosaura's veiled companion turns out to be Leonarda, Teolinda's sister. *Rosaura's tale* (told to Galatea and Florinda): The love between Rosaura and Grisaldo, her father's guest, had been troubled by her flirting with another guest, Artandro, an Aragonese gentleman who wanted to marry her. Grisaldo, discouraged, had gone off to marry a rich heiress chosen for him by his father. Rosaura had followed him in shepherdess' disguise. Meanwhile, Leonarda has been explaining her unexpected presence to her sister. *Leonarda's tale*: After Teolinda's departure, Leonarda had fallen in love with Galercio (Artidoro's identical twin), and had now come to look for him. Neither of the twins, however, had been seen in their village for some time. Silerio returns to his hermitage, and the shepherds and shepherdesses meet a group of travellers by the fountain: there is praise of country life (by Darinto, one of the travellers, and Damón), and a debate on love (Lenio speaking against, and Elicio for). It is discovered that the other traveller is Timbrio, and the ladies, Nísida and Blanca. They learn with joy that Silerio is not far, but Darinto hurries away at the news. Maurisa (the twins' young sister) rushes in calling for help. Galercio is in despair nearby, at the feet of inflexible Gelasia, dressed in nymph's garb, who scoffs at love. Lenio, finding her a person after his own "loveless" heart, goes off with her. Teolinda and Leonarda quarrel, each one insisting that the distressed suitor is *her* twin. Maurisa brings a message from Grisaldo to Rosaura: the secret marriage will take place two days hence. As dusk falls, Timbrio, Nísida, and Blanca are led to the hermitage.

Book V: During a joyful reunion at the hermitage, Silerio's story is now completed by *Timbrio's tale:* Nísida and Blanca, disguised as pilgrims, and Timbrio had been on the same ship to Spain unknown to one another until a happy recognition took place one night off the coast of Genoa. Soon after, they were captured by Turkish pirates, but a storm blew the pirates' galley aground on the Catalan coast. Thus rescued, Timbrio and the two sisters, accompanied by Darinto, a fellow traveller who was wooing Blanca, were travelling to Toledo.

Timbrio reveals to Silerio Blanca's secret love for him, and begs him to marry her. The next day is filled with incident. Darinto, giving up hope of Blanca, goes away for good. Elicio and Erastro are in a paroxysm of grief at the news that Galatea's father is marrying her off to a wealthy Lusitanian shepherd. She herself declares that this is against her will. Elicio offers to resort to force, if necessary, to prevent it. Artandro appears with an armed escort and carries off Rosaura to Aragon. Silerio agrees to marry Blanca, thus bringing the two friends' story to a happy end. Teolinda's affairs, on the other hand, take a disastrous turn: since Galercio is only interested in Gelasia, Leonarda decides to take Artidoro for herself, and using her resemblance to Teolinda, she tricks him into a formal betrothal to herself. Lauso recovers from his temporary infatuation and rejoices in being again "free." Lenio, on the other hand, has fallen with poetic justice for "loveless" Gelasia, and proclaims the power of love, a power further exemplified by old Arsindo, who determinedly dogs the footsteps of barely adolescent Maurisa. Telesio, the valley's "ancient priest" convenes all to the Valley of Cypresses, burial ground of eminent men, to commemorate the death of Meliso, the great shepherd-poet.

Book VI: Next morning, all proceed to the ceremony. Elicio praises the Tagus valley and Galatea, its fairest ornament. Memorial celebrations all day are followed at night by the supernatural appearance of Calliope, the muse of heroic poetry. In the *Song of Calliope* she sings the praises of one hundred contemporary Spanish poets. Next day, a gathering of all the main characters in a pleasant grove is interrupted by a commotion: Galercio attempts to drown himself in the Tagus under the eyes of unfeeling Gelasia, and is saved by two unknown shepherds. They are forerunners of Galatea's intended bridegroom, who will arrive within three days. In the last few pages, matters move swiftly to a head. Galatea begs Elicio to prevent the marriage. Over the next day and night, he calls in friends from outside, and works out strategies. As another day dawns, two groups of shepherds converge on the village, ready to fight the Portuguese bridegroom at Elicio's bidding. He prepares to plead with Galatea's father to cancel the marriage, failing which he will resort to violence. There the book ends abruptly, promising an early sequel "if this first part be received with a gentle will."

III   *Structure: The Plot and the Characters*

The design of *Galatea* conforms to the pattern set once and for all by Montemayor: a usually slender main plot in a pastoral setting, to which a number of contrasting, not necessarily pastoral, tales are linked in various ways.[3] In Cervantes, the main plot—the Elicio-Galatea relationship—is particularly tenuous. Almost to the very end (when Galatea's threatened marriage generates some developments), it remains no more than the opening situation of a possible story. The main burden of plot falls consequently almost wholly on the four inset tales. Like Gil Polo, Cervantes sought a degree of integration between the tales and the world of pastoral at the level of the action (in addition to their thematic relevance as illustrations of love cases), and it is fascinating to watch this first attempt of the great novelist at experimenting with different kinds of stories, varying interactions between their characters and those of the main setting, and changes of pace in telling and presentation. The events of Lisandro's story lie entirely in the past, and are recounted in the course of one single narrative. Rosaura's brief antecedents are also told in one recital, but the plot itself only begins to develop before the reader's eyes, in her scene with Grisaldo and her forcible abduction. This is clearly the initial phase of a story designed for further developments in the intended sequel.

Of the other two tales, Teolinda's is told in two sections. Important developments occur, but it is far from certain that the story can be regarded as closed when the novel ends: Leonarda, it is true, has tricked Artidoro into proposing marriage. But there are still all sorts of things Teolinda can do, such as try to extricate Artidoro (since the marriage has not yet taken place), or meditate some frightful revenge (not an unlikely course in a world where the kind of bloodshed seen in Lisandro's story can take place); or, taking a leaf out of her sister's book, she may decide that the wrong twin is better than none, and try to entice Galercio away from Gelasia. The situation is clearly open-ended. Silerio's and Timbrio's complex story is substantially independent and complete, but linked to the world of Elicio and Galatea by narrative devices, such as the gradual introduction of its characters, the telling of the tale in several stages and from different perspectives (partly by Silerio and partly by Timbrio), and the careful buildup of the happy ending.

As regards the materials and setting of the tales, only Teolinda's is relatively close to the pastoral world, being set (like Belisa's in Montemayor) in a farming village. Its theme, that of the comedy of errors resulting from the amorous adventures of identical twins, has a long literary ancestry, going back to Plautus. Cervantes adds complexity by introducing *two* pairs of identical siblings, and by having one of the girls betray her sister. The other three tales all concern persons of noble birth. Silerio's and Timbrio's is again a version of a theme with a long history in literature and folktale, the two-friends tale. The basic theme is that friendship is greater than love. In this case both claims are satisfied, and their story is the only one to end happily. In addition to the love interest and the demonstrations of friendship, the tale has all the typical appurtenances of the Greek romances: travels, storms, shipwrecks, pirates, duels, last-minute escapes, and so on. The setting, plot, and atmosphere of Lisandro's tale are those of an Italian *novella*, a genre in which Cervantes was particularly interested and which in the preface to his collection of *Exemplary Novels* he claimed to have introduced into Spanish letters. It is, in fact, a variation on the Romeo and Juliet theme. Rosaura's tale, on the other hand, seems to be Cervantes' own, designed to illustrate a point he was to make more than once in later writings, the dangers of ill-considered behavior, especially in matters of love. The characters are again of noble birth, but they are also part of Galatea's world, being the offspring of local landowners.

While these plots are being advanced, the pastoral world itself generates the beginnings of three other stories, exemplifying further love cases and providing material for a sequel. These are: (i) *Maurisa and Arsindo*—the old man falling in love with a young girl, a situation obviously fraught with dangers, and explored at length years later by Cervantes in his Exemplary Novel *El celoso extremeño (The Jealous Old Man from Extremadura)*; (ii) *Belisa and Marsilo*: In the Eclogue performed at Daranio's wedding, Marsilo has lamented Belisa's unresponsiveness. Much later, in Book VI, her appearance on the scene is mentioned in passing. Except for an exchange of songs, the relationship is not explored, but this establishes it as the germ of a future story; (iii) *Gelasia-Lenio-Galercio*: Here an inset tale merges with the world of Galatea and her shepherds to form the starting point of a new story. One character from Teolinda's tale (Galercio) and one from Galatea's village (Lenio) compete for the favors of Gelasia, and everyone becomes involved in trying to console them and preventing Galercio's suicide.

Galatea's essential structural device consists in combining a multiplicity of narrative strands to achieve a counterpoint of characters and events. The most distinctive element, (discussed below) is the use of suspense, heightened by interruptions, postponements, and alternations. This was to remain a favorite technique with Cervantes, to be deployed on a considerable scale in Part I of *Don Quixote*.

While the structure of *Galatea* thus adumbrates a fundamental technique of its author's mature work, the treatment of the characters is far from the psychological richness of the world of *Don Quixote*. In the pastoral novel, Cervantes examines a series of different love cases which are, by definition, typical. The characters acting out these situations are therefore largely types rather than individuals. They illustrate different attitudes to love, not so much as truly distinct alternatives, but rather as different points on what is basically the same emotional scale, which comprehends even the apparent antithesis between *enamorados* and *desamorados* (lovers and non-lovers). A *desamorado* is simply a potential *enamorado* who has yet to meet a sufficiently attractive object, as demonstrated by Lenio, who swings before our eyes from one to the other extreme. Lauso performs even more instructively by going through a similar process twice over in quick succession. To begin with, he is "free" Lauso, then he forms a mysterious yet violent attachment, but very soon thereafter he joyfully announces that all is now over—he has come to his senses again. Lauso is otherwise a marginal character. If, as may well be the case, he stands as a "mask" for Cervantes himself, to assign him a subsidiary role while occasionally allowing him the center of the stage would combine in the right degree a modicum of self-display with the necessary authorial modesty.

The other male lovers all come somewhere between the two extremes: they love faithfully and devotedly but, according to their
natures, they are impatient, and prone to brooding and despair
(Timbrio), or extravagant and suicidal (Galercio); some meekly accept
defeat (Mireno and Darinto), while others resort to force to assert
their rights (Artandro); some are easily swayed (Grisaldo, first by
Rosaura's feigned harshness, then by her emotional blackmail);
others rise above the trials of fate (Silerio, placing friendship before
love), while still others succumb to treachery (Lisandro) or deceit
(Artidoro, tricked into marrying the wrong sister). The midpoint of
the scale is occupied by Elicio: he endeavors to pursue the kind of
disinterested love he preaches to Erastro, and strives to avoid extremes of elation and despair, thus exemplifying Tirsi's theoretical
point: "the gifts of love, if used with temperance, are deserving of
perpetual praise, for the middle way has ever been as praised in all
things, as the extremes have been censured."

Among the female characters, Galatea represents the right attitude, the model to be followed, and she is explicitly praised in these
terms by Tirsi and Damón. She does not show her feelings, but
maintains an equable friendliness while discouraging familiarity. If
there is a danger, however, of losing the suitor through a serious
misunderstanding or some threatening change in the situation, then
it is proper, as Galatea does, to manifest one's own interest. The other
main female characters illustrate varying degrees of compliance with
the norm thus set. Nísida and her sister Blanca are equally exemplary, and Leónida is another character of the same caliber, though it
could be argued that her agreeing to the elopement is an act of
rashness which precipitates the tragedy. Prudent and circumspect as
they are during the courting period, however, these heroines are
capable of taking determined action once crises arise. Galatea does
not hesitate to ask Elicio for help, by violent means if necessary.
Nísida, accompanied by Blanca, sets off resolutely on a perilous quest
to look for Timbrio. Both Teolinda and Leonarda leave home and
family to go searching for their respective twin lovers. Rosaura pursues Artidoro and stages a dramatic suicide attempt. Cervantes'
women are a resolute lot. Sometimes, as in Leonarda's case, to the
point of ruthlessness: if she cannot have her own twin, she will take
her sister's. Leonarda, although a comparatively secondary figure, is
in fact one of the more individuated characters. Ostensibly, she is like
all other shepherdesses (or ladies) in love, but her actions reveal a
malevolent and self-seeking nature. She does her best to wreck her

sister's love affair with Artidoro, then falls in love with the nearest equivalent, his twin, and ends up by snatching the original Artidoro for herself. The mainspring of her actions, one concludes, is envy of her sister. And, with deliberate irony, the reader sees Leonarda mainly through the sister's eyes, unsuspecting until it is too late.

Gelasia is Lenio's counterpart, rather more steadfast in her "loveless" persuasion than he (though one may well suspect that she, in her turn, would have met with disaster in the sequel). Her opposite extreme is, of course, Rosaura, only too ready to flirt with more than one suitor at a time. Her lack of circumspection brings her and those around her nothing but trouble. She exemplifies a particular aspect of the code of conduct that Cervantes was, by implication, prescribing: excessive discouragement on the part of the young woman is unwise, as it may lead to the total alienation of the suitor. Both Grisaldo and Lauso are examples of this, and Tirsi formulates the point explicitly in his speech on love.

There are many secondary characters—shepherds, farmers, villagers, hunters, noblemen, pirates, sailors, highwaymen—enlivening the measured pastoral pace with a sense of teeming life and variety. Some of them are functional in terms of plot (e.g., Carino in Lisandro's tale, or Aurelio, Galatea's father). Others demonstrate yet further varieties of love cases, such as Arsindo chasing Maurisa and, especially, the "renowned" shepherds who perform the Eclogue at Daranio's wedding, illustrating four different kinds of heartbreak. Notable are Daranio and Silveria, the couple without problems, whose arranged marriage is celebrated to their own and (except for Mireno) everyone else's satisfaction. It is significant that Cervantes should have chosen to give it prominence in Book III, as a sort of practical counterpart to the ideological center of gravity of the novel, which follows immediately, in Book IV, in the disputation on love between Lenio and Tirsi.

One last question to be considered is the extent to which real persons are portrayed in some of the novel's characters. This consideration is of course no more relevant to literary quality here than it was in the case of Montemayor, but it is worth noting that Cervantes does not claim to be telling true stories. He uses the gentlemen-in-shepherds'-disguise argument for two purposes: first, to justify a certain latitude in the use of more elevated language and, especially, the introduction of "philosophical reasonings" (as he explains in the Preface), and second, as a means of introducing established fellow authors or possible patrons into the story in suitably complimentary ways. Many characters appear in this light in the pages of *Galatea*, but there are only three completely positive identifications. One is merely a passing allusion to Don John of Austria (under whom Cervantes had served at the battle of Lepanto) as Astraliano. The other two are poets: Diego Hurtado de Mendoza (1503–1575), who is the Meliso of the memorial ceremonies in the Valley of Cypresses, and Francisco de Figueroa (1536–1617?) who, as Tirsi, plays an important role in the novel.

The whole problem of identification has recently been taken a considerable step further by Geoffrey Stagg. In a closely argued piece of research,[4] he eschews the usual attempts at individual identification and demonstrates instead that there is a category of characters in the book who, on grounds of the status and fictional treatment accorded to them, may be regarded as "masks," or disguised characters. These include, in addition to the three just mentioned, Damón, Lenio, Larsileo, and Lauso. Stagg also shows that the group of "famous and well-known" poet-shepherds mentioned by Elicio in Book IV (Eranio, Siralvo, Filardo, Silvano, Lisardo, and both Matuntos, father and son) is included as a compliment to a friend and fellow pastoral author, Luis Gálvez de Montalvo (see Chapter 6), who contributed one of the three laudatory sonnets printed at the beginning of *Galatea*. Like Astraliano and Larsileo, the characters in this group are mentioned only once, and play no role in the novel. Damón and Lenio, on the other hand (like Tirsi), play significant roles in carrying the weight of the more ambitious statements on the philosophy of love: Lenio is Tirsi's opponent in the great debate on love in Book IV, and Damón holds the major speech against jealousy in Book III. As for Lauso, Stagg's examination of the evidence confirms that, as had already been suggested by others,[5] this may well be Cervantes' own "mask," donned not to portray any closely autobiographical experiences, but rather (following the custom of the time) as a poetic persona to take his fitting place in the literary establishment.

IV   *The Ideas: Theory of Love; Fortune, Time;*
Nature, Love, and Art; Shepherds and Courtiers;
Poetry, History, and Verisimilitude

Like Montemayor, Cervantes provides a Neoplatonic theoretical underpinning for his love stories, and turns to Italy for the ideas. The great debate on love in Book IV is largely based on the Neoplatonic love treatises of Bembo and Equicola, as will be seen later. Lenio, arguing against love, begins with a traditional definition of it as "desire of beauty," and draws a main distinction between good love (which pursues spiritual beauty) and bad love, which seeks the enjoyment of physical beauty as an end in itself. The latter is inevitably attended by suffering, and to be thoroughly condemned. As in Gil Polo, Cupid's traditional attributes are given a negative symbolical interpretation. Tirsi, defending love, denies that it is identical with desire. They are two different dispositions of the will. Love is of three kinds: pure, useful, and pleasant, and the important point is that *all three* are good at their own level. Pure love (of "heavenly things") obviously so; but useful love (of "earthly things, merry and transient, such as wealth, power and distinction") "being, as it is, natural, is not to be condemned"; nor is pleasant love ("of living corporeal beauty"), since "it is even more natural" than the useful kind. And whatever is natural cannot ultimately be contrary to God's design, since nature, in a famous Cervantine phrase, is defined as "God's steward" ("mayordomo de Dios"). Love of physical beauty has a twofold justification: philosophically, it can lead to the contemplation of higher things: in everyday life, guided by reason and regulated by "the holy bond of matrimony," it is the means of fulfilling the divine injunction "to have children, and perpetuate and spread mankind." Pursued in this manner, pleasant love is good amd involves the exercise of the four natural virtues: temperance, fortitude, justice, and prudence. Personal responsibility is asserted: those who blame love should blame themselves instead for making bad use of it. That even this kind of legitimate love often involves tears and sufferings is due to the degree of toil and effort required in the pursuit of any worthwhile aim (and sometimes to the folly of lovers who pitch their ambitions impossibly high). In any case, the joys of love are so intense as to outweigh any amount of suffering. Tirsi concludes with a positive reinterpretation of Cupid's attributes.

Cervantes' thinking was strongly colored by the Neoplatonic conceptions of his day, but he was not content merely to repeat a number of commonplaces. He took a major concept of Renaissance Neoplatonism (the power and splendor of nature and its workings) and harnessed it to the justification of the Neoplatonists' lower kinds of love in terms which satisfy the claims of both Christianity and common sense. The drift of Tirsi's argument strikes a note not found in its sources and which seems, in the pastoral context, distinctly Cervantes' own. The stress is on ethics and moral responsibility, as in Gil Polo. But, unlike him, Cervantes is not writing to demonstrate a philosophical conviction. His attitude is one of realistic acceptance of human nature and (for all of the standard pastoral gestures) of its practical implications in the world of everyday experience. This explains the repeated injection of common-sense considerations in illustrating the consequences of lovers' actions. In this context, Daranio's and Silveria's wedding is seen in its proper perspective as the coming to fruition of the useful and pleasant loves; Mireno, the impecunious, disappointed "romantic" lover goes off, and the wedding proceeds merrily, with no hint of unwillingness on the part of Silveria, whose chosen bridegroom is not only a rich but also a good-looking young man. The Eclogue performed as a wedding entertainment shows a variety of contrasting unhappy love situations, perhaps as a reminder of the many pitfalls that beset the pursuit of prosperity and happiness. But the pursuit itself goes robustly on.

The Eclogue is the occasion for the immediately following speech by Damón condemning jealousy as the worst (because the least justified) of the four kinds of love suffering presented. The other conditions (death, absence, refusal) have objective correlatives. But jealousy is made up by and from the lover's own mind, and is inexhaustible. Yet its greater suffering does not argue greater love, but rather impertinent curiosity about the object of one's passion, and lack of confidence in oneself.[6] In fact (using an argument which has already been encountered in Gil Polo), jealousy in love is like fever in a patient: a sign of a diseased, not a healthy condition.

In the love debate, Lenio warns that human love entails suffering because it is subject to *fortune* and *chance*, that is to say, to change. In the nature of things, change takes place in and is often brought about by the passage of *time*. An awareness of this fact lies, in one way or another, at the root of all love literature. Each pastoral author comes to terms with it in his own way. Montemayor stresses the effects of the passage of time, either in natural duration (Sireno's prolonged absence) or symbolically accelerated (Felicia's potion). Gil Polo, on the other hand, with his ethical stress on personal responsibility and consistent behavior, makes the changes dependent on psychological preparation and correct understanding. Cervantes, echoing Montemayor, begins by placing the three key concepts before the reader. (The novel opens with Elicio suffering from the adversities of fortune and love, sharpened by the passage of time.) But he does not dwell long in that elegiac mood, and proceeds to develop a view of personal responsibility for one's own affairs. This is, essentially, very close to Gil Polo's but, consistent with Cervantes' keen awareness of the ambiguities of human nature, tempered by a healthy measure of qualification and common sense. The fact that he is using the current Petrarchan vocabulary of love poetry entails the inevitable references to fate, destiny, signs, and the influence of the stars, as well as to fortune or chance,[7] but these elements are used with due regard for the motivations inherent in character and situation.

The fourth important concept in the opening passage on Elicio is that of *nature* which, as we have just seen, plays an important function in Cervantes' philosophy. The question of the relative roles and mutual relationship of nature and art was one of the crucial philosophical topics of the age, and writing a pastoral novel represented, in itself, a contribution to the ongoing debate. A contribution which, in the case of Cervantes, must be seen as one of the facets of the fundamental concern which was later to inform *Don Quixote*: the theme of truth and illusion, with its infinitely complex system of shifting relationships. Cervantes explored this theme on repeated occasions, and from various angles, of which we shall here consider another two in addition to the theme of nature *versus* art: the Aristotelian contrast between poetry and history (in relation to the theory and practice of literature), and the contrast between shepherds and courtiers (a topic which runs through much of Spanish Golden Age writing, and is really part of the larger nature-and-art issue).

"In mediaeval scholasticism, with the rediscovery of the Aristotelian concept of Nature, God's exceptional Grace is made to serve as the antithetical term. But in Renaissance humanism, it is God, not Man, who is subsumed under Nature; and the antithetical term is no longer divine Grace but human Art."[8] E. L. Rivers' formulation cannot be bettered for clarity and concision. The Renaissance concept of nature, though always subject in theory to the power of God, tended not infrequently to be identified, more or less implicitly, with that power itself. As the great scholar Américo Castro showed in his fundamental study of Cervantes' thought,[9] the old scholastic term, *natura naturans*, had now a new ring of independence, or almost: nature as Creator. Producing, pervading, and sustaining *natura naturata*, the natural world of concrete experience. But man, the other pole of the dialectic pair, was also felt to enjoy a greater autonomy. He was a part of the created world, but also (as Cervantes might have punned) apart from it, standing to it in a subject-object relationship which gave scope for the creative exercise upon it of his human knowledge and skills, of his art.

From the point of view of the Church, the antithesis, thus formulated, had serious unorthodox implications which many authors, especially in Italy, did not fail to explore. But it could also be put to fruitful use within an unexceptionably orthodox framework. This is Cervantes' position. Nature is, quite explicitly, God's steward—i.e., the executor and not, in any ultimate sense, the originator of the design. The justification of the lower kinds of love on the grounds that they are natural is immediately purged of any unorthodox overtones by its placing in a firmly Christian context. There is a delicate balancing of the connotations of the term "natural" when predicated of human inclinations. Since the Fall of Man, to seek means of subsistence and comfort and to procreate (the "useful" and "pleasant" loves) are activities natural to man, both because they correspond to his inner nature, and because they are the "natural"—i.e., sensible, correct—response to the situation in which he finds himself. And art, in its most general sense, is the exercise of the whole range of human skills deployed by man in the process of coping with this situation.

A cooperative relationship develops between man and nature, in which the antithesis is resolved, art combined with, not opposed to, nature. Cervantes is not the only author of his time tending toward this resolution, but he is the one who places it most visibly before the reader's eyes, notably in the praise of the Tagus valley at the beginning of Book VI. Here, the wealth of nature and the agricultural activities of man are shown to blend in a positive, mutually enhancing relationship: the life-giving river meanders through the tilled fields, its banks are adorned (not defaced or polluted) by numerous villages and rich farms; there are tall waterwheels to convey water into ditches for the irrigation of distant fields, and these are singled out for praise, in deliberately epic-sounding language: "the tall wheels, whose continued motion draws up water from the river depths and abundantly bathes the far distant fields." They illustrate the immediately preceding, explicit formulation of the nature-art synthesis: "And the industry of the [valley's] dwellers has achieved so much that nature, united with art, is turned artificer and connatural to art, and of the two together there has arisen a third nature which I would not know by what name to call." E. L. Rivers comments: "Cervantes' fusion of Nature and Art might perhaps be called either 'Natura artifex' or 'Ars naturans' ".[10] The harmonious integration of opposites in "third nature" is symbolized in musical terms in the performance of Meliso's obsequies where the quiet sobbing of the shepherdesses, the shepherds' sad music, and the merry song of the birds "formed all together such a striking and sorrowful harmony as was beyond the praise of any tongue."

The fusion nature-art, however, is something that occurs only at certain times, or at certain levels. At others, the straight antithesis is presented in the customary way. The relationship between human music-making and birdsong, for instance, is sometimes left unresolved, as in the scene, in Book VI, where the birds' "wonderful unlearned harmony" is contrasted with the shepherds' instruments and "sonorous voices." When contrasted with the world of plants and animals, the shepherds represent the human world of artifice. More frequently, however, the terms of the comparison are different: the shepherds, regarded as an integral part of the natural world of pastoral, are contrasted with courtiers or townspeople, invariably to the detriment of the latter, in accordance with the topic (recurrent in literature ever since Horace's "Beatus ille") of the idealization of country life. The topic was, by definition, inherent in the pastoral genre, and Cervantes did not fail to give it due place in *Galatea*. The paradox, central to the pastoral genre, of presenting "natural" shepherds as highly sensitive, always eloquent, and often erudite, characters, made Cervantes uncomfortable. His views on literature were predominantly neo-Aristotelian,[11] and one of the essential features of neo-Aristotelian literary theory was the distinction between "poetry" and "history," and its corollary, the need for plausibility, or verisimilitude, as it was currently termed, in the former.

Now it was essentially implausible that shepherds would utter subtle thoughts in flowing language. The dilemma, in E.C. Riley's precise formulation, was simply: "How did one invest the novel with the beautiful and desirable ornaments of poetry without sacrificing that matter-of-fact credibility so essential to it?"[12] At the level of language and style, Cervantes not only took advantage of the customary character-in-shepherds'-disguise disclaimer in the preface, but also took pains to stress the point from time to time in the body of the book. But verisimilitude must extend beyond stylistic propriety, to comprise plot and incident. This was easily enough done in the inset stories of intrigue and adventure, and there are plenty of instances showing that Cervantes took trouble to furnish motives and justifications. Even the story of the two pairs of twins (which, being set in a farming village, comes perilously close to the pastoral paradox) is maintained, in Teolinda's narration, at a remarkably non-idealized level and, significantly, contains only two brief poems.

The world of pastoral literary convention, on the other hand, poses problems. The boldest course is by and large the best: to operate openly, as Sannazaro did, and Montemayor very nearly, at the level of self-consistent literary artifice, with its own kind of verisimilitude, without attempting to bolster it up with realistic detail. But this is something Cervantes could not quite bring himself to do. Not so much on account of his neo-Aristotelian critical convictions, but because it went against the grain of those particular gifts that he was to put to superlative use in some of the *Exemplary Novels* and, above all, in *Don Quixote*: the ear for the cadences of everyday speech, the eye for the telling detail, and the quick sense for the absurdity inherent in all kinds of situations. The latter bubbles up irrepressibly on at least one occasion: Galercio, attempting to drown himself in despair at Gelasia's disdain, is found in a most undignified position, as his sister and Teolinda struggle to pull him out: half in the river, head under water, legs in the air, and kicking out to make the girls let go of his feet.

Pastoral novels did include, as a formal part of the tradition, a few references to the material aspects of shepherds' lives: pauses for food and rest, general references to basic pastoral activities, etc. These have sometimes been mistakenly hailed as traces of "realism." They are nothing of the sort, but Cervantes did his best to take advantage of these traditional aids to verisimilitude, and endeavored to enhance them by adding circumstantial information on matters such as timing and topography that lent an air of actuality and precision to the story. He also made an attempt to introduce a real "rustic shepherd" (as a foil to Elicio) in the character of Erastro, but did not manage to sustain his rusticity. Erastro's kin are not the shepherds out in the fields, but the "rustics" of Juan del Encina's and Lucas Fernández' eclogues, and his presence merely represents an additional strand of literary convention. Well-intentioned touches of this kind only serve, in the final analysis, to point up the gap between the ideal and the actual. Cervantes' efforts to achieve a compromise between an all-out ideal world and one of mainly literary actuality are self-defeating. Things which are perfectly acceptable in a self-validating ideal world become upsettingly improbable when measured against implied standards of everyday reality. The result is a lesser, not a greater, degree of credibility. The reader who accepted without difficulty the existence of nymphs, wild men, and supernatural palaces in Montemayor, is disturbed here by much milder events such as the stately procession of shepherds, gravely marching through the countryside and playing solemn music, as they escort Daranio, crowned with "a garland of honeysuckle and various other flowers," through the fields and meadows of a no-longer-unequivocal pastoral world.

V *Literary Form and Technique: The Use of Suspense; Description; Praise of Spanish Writers*

The multiplicity of plots typical of the Spanish pastoral novel inevitably raises the question of how best to knit the material together. We have seen that Montemayor and Gil Polo both think in terms of a broad, organizing structure in which each tale is a distinct building-block, though they differ in the degree of mutual involvement between the inset stories and the pastoral mainstream. Cervantes, on the other hand, enjoys the challenge of juggling with several stories at once. To hold them together he relies not so much on structure as on the use of techniques that will fulfill the basic requirement of the storyteller's craft: to foster the reader's desire to know "what comes next." To this end he uses, in particular, surprise and suspense (the classic devices of the Greek romances) and a good deal of violent action.

To begin with a murder and end with an imminent threat of disturbance of the peace is hardly what one expects of a pastoral novel. Yet violence runs like a red thread through the texture of *Galatea*. The stories of Lisandro and the two friends are, of course, full of it. But the peace of the pastoral world itself is frequently shaken by acts of violence, attempted or performed, sometimes as a carryover from one of the inset stories (as Carino's killing, or Rosaura's kidnapping), at other times as the outward manifestation of violent states of mind in the pastoral characters themselves—quarrels, fights, attempted suicides, and the like. From the mysterious murder that shatters the shepherds' bucolic peace at the beginning, to Elicio and his friends marching on Aurelio's house to deliver their ultimatum at the end, violence and anxious expectation are frequently in the air, and suspense is heightened by means of hints, interruptions, and gradual revelations.

Unfortunately, the nature of the pastoral novel is not such as to furnish a medium in which such a technique can flourish. The narrative thrust generated by suspense is constantly being held up by the introduction of formal lyrics and debates, and the disproportionately bulky section devoted to the Valley of Cypresses and the song of Calliope constitutes, even more than its equivalents in Montemayor and Gil Polo, an evident stumbling block. On the whole, the strictures applied by some critics to *Galatea*, and still too often unthinkingly repeated concerning its alleged narrative weaknesses, have been vastly exaggerated. To say that "there seems to be no attempt at plot or connected narrative" or, more cautiously, that the "subplots are so varied and numerous that on occasion they seem to constitute an impenetrable morass" [13] merely argues a hasty reading. *Galatea* deserves more than that, and repays it richly. But it *is* a long work (twice as long as either the first *Diana* or *Diana enamorada*); it brings together a great deal of varied material, and it is true that Cervantes' skill in organizing the mass of material was not equal to the task in this his first novel. The narrative devices on which he mainly relied for control, successful as they are at many points, did not entirely suffice to provide the necessary degree of cohesion.

Cervantes, not unlike Gil Polo, was primarily concerned with deeds, their motives and consequences, with action rather than contemplation. Not unnaturally, therefore, there is little description in *Galatea*. But no pastoral novel was complete without a few set-pieces, and Cervantes was not one to neglect this possibility of displaying his talents. Significantly, however, four of the five passages of this kind in *Galatea* are found in the inset tales of adventure, and portray highly dramatic situations: Leónida's ambush and murder in Lisandro's story; the pirates' night attack on the coastal town, the storm at sea, and the capture of the Spanish ship by pirates in Timbrio's and Sileno's tales. Only one major set-piece deals with an entirely peaceful scene, located in the pastoral world. And even this one involves a lot of action, although of a harmless kind, since it deals with the bustle of preparations in the village on the morning of Daranio's and Silveria's wedding. In all situations, Cervantes introduces concrete factual touches and circumstantial detail (e. g., the exact tactics of an ambush, the mechanics of a naval manoeuver, or the topography of a valley) to enhance the sense of immediacy. This can also be observed in another type of description indispensable in a pastoral novel—the pastoral setting itself, the *locus amoenus*. This is stylized and abbreviated in presentation, but with sufficient detail to blend sights, sounds, and scents into a harmonious scene. The culmination of nature description, however, is Elicio's praise of the Tagus valley which opens Book VI. This not only illustrates, as mentioned above, an important ideological point, but it also takes up another stock theme of the pastoral novel, the "praise of places" (as found in Montemayor's description of the Mondego valley, and Gil Polo's praise of Valencia). It is an ambitious display piece constructed with care, involving literary and mythological allusions, and ending with a neat transition to the praise of Galatea. Timbrio is left full of admiration, and one cannot escape the feeling that Cervantes hoped the reader would be similarly moved.

Finally, a word must be said about dawn descriptions, [14] one of the perennial topics of poetry, which with Sannazaro had found its way into the pastoral novel. Both Montemayor and Gil Polo had used dawn descriptions, though sparingly. Cervantes, on the other hand, consistently resorted to them as a decorative element in *Galatea*. The novel extends over a period of ten days, and each day's business punctiliously begins with the rising of the sun. In only one case, the last dawn at the very end, is this a simple allusion to "the morning having come." Everywhere else, the opportunity is seized to produce a piece of ornamental writing, mostly in mythological terms (with references to Aurora or Phoebus).

VI *The Language: Prose and Poetry*

It is one of the commonplaces of Cervantine criticism that, at least in *Don Quixote* and the *Exemplary Novels*, Cervantes was a master of prose style. *Galatea*, too, though so often criticized for weaknesses of construction, has harvested a fair measure of recognition for its stylistic qualities. An adequate analysis of its prose style cannot be attempted here, but a few distinguishing characteristics may be briefly touched upon. [15]

Like all authors of his time, Cervantes was writing against the theoretical background of the classical division (going back to the *Rhetorica ad Herennium*) into three styles: the grand style of epic or tragedy, the low style of comedy, and an intermediate or mixed style. The latter had, since Sannazaro, become recognized as suitable for the pastoral novel. It was, in Riley's words, "in theory more simple than magnificent, but elegant and decorated, not crude, corresponding to the lyrical style in poetry." [16] It reflected, of course, the fact that the kind of cultivated shepherds portrayed in pastoral required a more elevated medium than the low style reserved for the rustic shepherds and other low characters of comedy. In *Galatea*, Cervantes is not bound by hard and fast divisions, but moves freely between different stylistic levels, as occasion and the type of action demand. In this he follows and develops the approach already observed in Gil Polo. But where Gil Polo endeavors to be functionally unobtrusive, Cervantes wants to be seen to operate effectively over the full range. He makes a convincing enough display of elevated style, with deliberate use of rhetorical devices (e.g., in the dawn descriptions, the praise of the Tagus valley, the description of the Valley of Cypresses, the impassioned pleadings of lovers, etc.), but to see him at his best we must turn to the action and storytelling.

Here we find a well-fashioned, flexible medium being competently put to a variety of uses: the swift, economical description of Carino's killing; the lively vignette of the hunted hare; the sure touch (theatrical in flavor) with which Erastro is shown, comically losing his temper with Lenio and having to be physically prevented from resorting to blows to settle an argument about love. The most striking feature of Cervantes' prose and one which he was to develop in later works is the easy, leisurely flow of the language, even where scenes of violent action are being described. This is achieved by broad rhythms and prolonged periods and by characteristic syntactic devices. One of these is the use of sequences of adjective-noun groups with the adjective preceding the noun, functioning, in Spanish syntax, as a general epithet, for purposes of rhythm, color, or poetic ornament. [17] Another device, so frequent as to constitute practically a mannerism, is the recourse to demonstrative pronouns and to the pronominal use of adjectives, to establish referential systems which knit together the clause structure and sometimes serve also to suggest subtle shifts in viewpoint or relationship by playing on different connotations of the same antecedent. [18] In experimenting with a whole gamut of stylistic devices, Cervantes was not only seeking that "mastery in the skillful use of the resources of eloquence" which he defined as a writer's goal in the Preface to *Galatea*, but was already beginning to develop the technique of contrasting styles which was to come to fruition in *Don Quixote*.

Unlike Cervantes' prose, his poetry seldom, if ever, rises above a mediocre level, a fact of which he himself was painfully aware. Yet he was always fascinated by the (to him) unwieldy medium, and in *Galatea* he took full advantage of the genre's characteristic requirements to insert a large amount of poetic compositions. He used all the established Italianate forms (as might be expected in a follower of the Petrarchan poetic tradition) but did not for this reason turn away from traditional native meters. Though in substantially lesser numbers, *Galatea* also contains the usual range of these. The contents of the poems are completely standard for the time and genre, with a good measure of Neoplatonic ideas and imagery (see Timbrio's verse letter to Nísida at the beginning of Book III) and the inevitable lengthy laudatory poem, the *Song of Calliope*, praising one hundred contemporary writers (ranging from the eminent to the very obscure) in 111 *octavas reales*.

Stylistically, there is a good deal of use of the techniques which had been typical of fifteenth-century Spanish lyrics, working with conceits, antitheses, and parallelism, as well as the Petrarchan themes and techniques from Italy. Among the latter, the techniques known as "correlation" and "multiple enumeration" (in which a number of key concepts are introduced first singly or in individual groups, and then recapitulated together)[19] could not but appeal to him. Their semantic and syntactic structures were a highly suitable vehicle for his own sense of human affairs as a complex web of multiple relationships, and he used them accordingly. Elicio's opening lament "Mientras que al triste lamentable acento" ("Whilst to the sad and mournful lamentation") is a typical example.

Cervantes took evident pains to write poetry that would be, as the situation demanded, sonorous, moving, or witty. But his gift was too slender in that direction; try as he would, he succeeded only occasionally in coining an arresting image or giving striking expression to well-worn thoughts. And he was not helped by conscientious but awkward craftsmanship. Some of the compositions are pleasing enough, but taken as a whole, in *Galatea* as elsewhere, Cervantes' poetry is no more than second-rate.

VII *Literary Sources*[20]

Not enough is known about Cervantes' cultural background but, in spite of the fact that he was not a formally qualified scholar, his writings show that he was well-read, inspired by a highly active intellectual curiosity, and capable of exercising a discrimination both subtle and self-reliant. He took ideas and materials from many sources and used them freely, hardly concerned with verifying, and not at all with acknowledging, sources or references, but only with supplying whatever was necessary to his own creative purpose. That he turned very frequently to Italian sources is not surprising in an author who had spent several years of his life in Italy and had been able to acquire an intimate personal knowledge of the language and literature. The great love debate in Book IV is a case in point. Its two main sources are Pietro Bembo's *Gli Asolani* (1505, though Cervantes seems to have used the second (1530) or third (1555) edition) for

Lenio's speech, and Mario Equicola's *Libro di natura de amore* (1525) for Tirsi's. No sources have been found for some of the materials in the speeches, but they contain at any rate nothing that (despite what was long believed) derives directly from Leone Ebreo.[21] Literary materials of Italian origin are plentiful both in the narrative and the lyrical parts of *Galatea*. The plot of Lisandro's tale, for instance, is a version of the Romeo and Juliet story which the *novelle* of Luigi da Porto (1524) and Matteo Bandello (1554) had made popular throughout Europe. Silverio's and Timbrio's story takes up an old theme of Arabic origin, the two-friends tale, the most famous version of which was found in Boccaccio's *Decameron* (Tito and Gisippo, X, 8), although here Cervantes already had an example nearer home in the version inserted by Alonso Pérez in his *Diana* (see Ch. 6), and may well have been acquainted with other Spanish versions as well. Alonso Pérez had combined the two-friends tale with another much-repeated motif, that of the twins, which had its origins in Plautus' play *Menaechmi*. And interestingly enough, Cervantes makes this the basis of Teolinda's story.

In the poetry, the Italian influence is both pervasive and diffuse. The channels through which it could reach Cervantes, both directly and through many Spanish poets from Garcilaso onward, are manifold, and a general acknowledgment of the fact must suffice for the present purpose. Cervantes was very much in the stream of sixteenth-century Petrarchan poetry in Spain. It is significant that it was to Francisco de Figueroa, a leader of the Petrarchan school, that he gave an important role in *Galatea*, as Tirsi, the acknowledged great poet-shepherd, and upholder of the right view of love in the debate. Calliope's prose speech introducing her *Song* gives a useful indication of the names that came to Cervantes' mind as part of the mainstream poetic heritage. The list contains no surprises, and falls into three groups: poets of classical antiquity, the Italians, and some Spaniards (of the very recent past). The Italians are Petrarch, Dante, and Ariosto, in that order. The classical poets include Homer, Virgil, Ennius, Catullus, Horace, and Propertius. Obviously, this is principally a bringing together of suitably impressive names. Since Cervantes was no classical scholar, we need not expect to find in *Galatea* any but the kind of topics that were the common currency of Renaissance poetry. Foremost among these, of course, is the imitation of Horace's *Beatus ille* concluding Damón's song "El vano imaginar de nuestra mente" ("The vain imaginings of our mind") in Book IV.

The Spanish poets mentioned in Calliope's introduction are Boscán, Garcilaso, Castillejo, Torres Naharro, Francisco de Aldana, Acuña, and Diego Hurtado de Mendoza (the Meliso whose death is being commemorated). It is interesting that, apart from Torres Naharro, the oldest one (d. 1524), and Castillejo, all the others are in the mainstream of Petrarchan poetry, reflecting Cervantes' general commitment to the Italianate school. To these we may add the three foremost exponents of Petrarchism who are given particular prominence in the *Song*: Luis de León, (1527?–1591, Pedro Laynez (1538?–1584), and Francisco de Figueroa (1536–1617). But the great master, for Cervantes as for so many others, is of course Garcilaso. Like Gil Polo before him, but less successfully, Cervantes strives to emulate the deceptive simplicity of Garcilaso's musical flow. And, again like Gil Polo, he follows the fashion of studding his verses by way of homage, and signal to the initiated, with quotations or near-quotations from Garcilaso's works.[22]

As for Sannazaro, the presence of the originator of the genre is of course felt and acknowledged (e.g., in the mention of the river Sebeto in a list of famous rivers), and there are imitations both of basic motifs (e.g., the holding of memorial or funeral celebrations) and of detail, such as the opening lines of the *canción* "Oh, alma venturosa" ("Oh, blessed soul").[23] On the whole, however, the extent of Cervantes' debt to Sannazaro, believed at one time to be considerable, has been found on closer examination to be remarkably modest.[24]

VIII   *Pastoral, Literature and Life*

Cervantes' attitude to pastoral has been the subject of much discussion. Was *Galatea* simply a beginner's effort, couched in a fashionable convention which he would outgrow, or was the pastoral mode a lasting part of his intellectual and artistic makeup? His own writings provide ammunition for both views. There is, in the *Voyage to Parnassus*, the ironically worded catalogue of lyrical forms suitable for use and abuse in pastoral novels. And there is, in particular, the much-quoted passage from the exemplary novel *Colloquy of the Dogs* in which Berganza, the sheepdog, sharply contrasts the coarse existence of real shepherds with that of "shepherds in books," and concludes "that all these books are things dreamed and well written for the amusement of the idle, and not at all true." On the other hand, Cervantes manifested, throughout his life, a particular affection for *Galatea*, referring to it with modest, but firm authorial pride in that same ironical *Voyage to Parnassus*, and renewing at least four times in the course of his life (even when already on his deathbed) the promise to write a sequel.[25] While this could still be dismissed as an indulgent fondness for the work of his youth, Cervantes' repeated use of pastoral materials in later works indicates a deeper involvement. There is pastoral in one of his late plays, *The House of Jealousy*, and in his posthumous *Persiles and Sigismunda*.

But the most significant evidence by far comes from *Don Quixote*, where the pastoral thread runs through the texture of the whole novel.[26] The knight's library contains, as is well known, pastoral novels (including *Galatea*) as well as books of chivalry, and they are also subjected to the priest's and barber's inquisition (Part I, Ch. 6). Shortly before his death, Don Quixote (fulfilling his niece's earlier fears) decides to turn pastoral, the idea being suggested by his earlier encounter with a group of ladies and gentlemen who were amusing themselves by performing verse eclogues by Garcilaso and Camões in a suitably sylvan spot (Part II, Chs. 58, 67). This "new pastoral Arcadia" both harks back to the Renaissance courtly origins of the genre (when Boccaccio would write verse eclogues such as the *Ninfale Fiesolano* as a courtly entertainment), and points forward to its ultimate decay—prettified and voided of all meaning—as a society game in the eighteenth century.

But at some points in *Don Quixote*, encounters of substance occur between pastoral literature and life, in particular in the tale of Grisóstomo and Marcela (Part I, Chs. 11–14). There pastoral reality and the pastoral dream are briefly juxtaposed, and the world of poetic fiction is shown to have very definite effects on the life and death of quite real human beings.[27] In a context of ordinary, down-to-earth shepherds, Marcela (the rich farmer's daughter who does not want to marry) and Grisóstomo, the young country gentleman just back from University, act out a tragic pastoral resulting in his love-death (probably by suicide, though this is left deliberately vague). The situation is highly artificial—like the ladies and gentlemen of *Don Quixote's* encounter, they are playing at shepherds—but thoroughly real in the total commitment of Marcela to her freedom, and of Grisóstomo to his love. Lived out, in his case, quite literally to its ultimate consequence.[28] This example of pastoral in action demonstrates the reality of the inner world, which is here acted out in terms of literary convention. It is ushered in by Don Quixote's speech on the Golden Age, addressed to an audience of uncomprehending goatherds. This is one of the master-strokes of the mature Cervantes: while pointing up the irrelevance of the Golden Age myth to the lives of actual shepherds, it places that root element, the longing for the Golden Age, firmly before the reader, thus alerting him to the fact that there is a double frame of reference in operation: the immediate world of the goatherds sitting round Don Quixote, *and* the ideal world of pastoral. With some oversimplification, one could say that the contrast is that between the world of purely physical reality, and the world of feelings and ideas by which human beings live and die, and which is, therefore, in human terms, if anything more intensely real than the other. The resulting episode is, as Avalle-Arce puts it, "a majestic orchestration of Cervantes' ever pressing theme of ambivalent reality." [29] It is in this light that the oft-quoted criticism of pastoral in the *Colloquy of the Dogs* must be seen. Cervantes is not condemning "things dreamed and well-written" because they are "not at all true." He is simply, once again, illustrating the Aristotelian contrast between the "universal truth" of art and the "particular truth" of historical fact. If Berganza the dog's dictum is to be taken as a condemnation, *all* works of imaginative literature, and not just pastoral, are being condemned, which is patently absurd. The flea-bitten, unwashed Juanica of Berganza's experience does not invalidate the ideal Galatea of pastoral. Like Sancho and Don Quixote, they are the two poles of one single universe. *Galatea* marks the beginning of Cervantes' attempt at a synthesis which, denying neither, would encompass both, and which his mature vision eventually achieved in *Don Quixote*.

CHAPTER 5

Lope Felix De Vega Carpio:
Arcadia, Prosas y Versos . . .
con una Exposición de los Nombres
Historicos y Poéticos
(Arcadia, *Proses and Verses . . .*
With an Explanation of the
Historical and Poetical Names).[1]

I *The Author*

LOPE Félix de Vega Carpio (1562–1635) is another figure that
needs no introduction. His dramatic masterpieces (such as *Peribañez, Fuenteovejuna, The Knight of Olmedo, Punishment Without Revenge*) are world-famous, and his facility as a playwright who wrote literally hundred of plays is common knowledge. What is perhaps less generally known outside Spain is that he was equally prolific in the nondramatic field: he poured out a flood of lyric poetry, verse epics, mythological poems, devotional poetry, and versified literary theory. His prose output was also substantial: four novels of considerable length, and a number of short stories. The first of the novels and, in fact, the first of his works to appear in print, (in 1598), was *Arcadia*. (His other, religious-pastoral novel, *The Shepherds of Bethlehem* [1612] will be briefly discussed in Chapter 6). Most, if not all, of *Arcadia* was written during Lope de Vega's period as a member of the household of Antonio Alvarez de Toledo, Duke of Alba. This was a peaceful interlude, both emotionally and materially, in his turbulent existence. Banished from Madrid for his libels against the family of his former mistress Elena Osorio, he had returned secretly to elope with

seventeen-year-old Isabel de Urbina, his first wife; had sailed with
the Armada (1588); lived in Valencia for a couple of years; and finally,
in 1591/92, found patronage and brief security in the ducal court at
Alba de Tormes. This he left for Madrid in 1595, when his banishment was lifted. His young wife had died in childbirth the previous
autumn.

II *The Novel*

Prologue: In writing this tale of love in high spheres, the author also
laments his own misfortunes. The literary precedent of Virgil's eclogues justifies the characters' elevated speech and behavior.
Book I: Set in the countryside around Mount Menalus in classical
Arcadia, the tale will show the progress of noble Anfriso (said to be
descended from Jupiter) from the tribulations of love to the mental
peace of *desengaño* or disillusionment. He and Belisarda love each
other, but she has been promised in marriage to wealthy Salicio. She
dreams that Anfriso loves another, which leads to a lovers' argument
and reconciliation. Galafrón and Leriano, two unsuccessful suitors,
discuss Belisarda's and Anfriso's outstanding qualities. Isbella and
her lover Menalca quarrel about Olimpio, her former lover. To
amuse her and others (Leonisa, Alcino, Isbella, and Olimpio), Menalca invents a tale. *Crisalda and Alasto, Part I*: Alasto the giant, son of
Jupiter and a nymph, wooed Crisalda the shepherdess. The tale is
interrupted by the arrival of Celio, mad with jealousy, who has to be
controlled by force. Old Tirso points to this warning of love's consequences. Benalcio, "a learned mathematician," tells a tale showing
the deceitfulness of appearances. *Jupiter, the Red Rose, and the
Green Snake*: All beings were bringing presents to Jupiter, according
to their nature. The viper came last, with a red rose in its poison fangs
bringing destruction under the guise of beauty. In punishment,
Jupiter turned it into a constellation, and made thorns grow on roses.
Celso sings the story of Celio's ill-fated love, and the struggling
madman is hauled off to the village by Cardenio "the rustic" and the
others.
Book II: Night scene: Anfriso sadly bids Belisarda farewell. His rivals'
machinations have succeeded in getting him sent to Mount Lycaeum.
His friend Silvio watches over Belisarda, while Galafrón and Leriano
vainly organize entertainments to amuse and court her. The summer
solstice pilgrimage is held to the temple of Pales, goddess of flocks.
Belisarda's disappointed suitors discourse on tears and jealousy.

Menalca resumes *Crisalda and Alasto, part II*: The credulous giant, long deceived by Crisalda's terrified temporizing, had at last learned of her wedding to Orfindo on the day itself, and wrathfully descended upon the village. Pacified by the promise that she would be handed over to him, he had joined the banquet, where he was made drunk, bound, and hacked to death. Next day, they plundered his cave. The rites of Pales completed, the shepherds visit a cave containing three empty sepulchres reserved to great men of the future: Gonzalo Girón; the Marquess of Santa Cruz; Fernando Alvarez de Toledo, third Duke of Alba. Belisarda leaves for Cyllene with her father Clorinardo. Olimpio, still smarting under Isbella's slight, seeks solace in following Belisarda, while Silvio sends news to Anfriso, so that he may secretly visit her.

Book III: Pining Anfriso receives the news from Silvio, together with letters from Olimpio, who falsely claims to be watching over Belisarda, while in fact pressing his unwelcome suit on her. Anfriso secretly joins her in Cyllene, but his presence soon becomes generally known. After a period of constant entertainments (with debates on love, on beauty, and on constancy), he is again forced to leave. He goes to Italy where, on a stormy night, he meets Dardanio the magician and is shown his cave, with its effigies of famous figures of antiquity and Spanish national heroes. At his request, Dardanio magically flies him back to Cyllene for a secret glimpse of Belisarda. He witnesses Olimpio's heavy courting, misconstrues her reaction, and wrongly concludes that she is unfaithful. Wafted back to Italy in a paroxysm of jealousy, he returns to Mount Menalus intent on revenge. His enemies spread false rumors which harden his resolve. On Silvio's advice, he courts and wins Anarda, to the despair of Enareto, hitherto her lover. Life is an endless round of parties, with exchanges of presents, song contests, a literary debate, and the performance of an *Eclogue of Montano and Lucindo*.

Book IV: Anfriso leaves to visit his dying mother. Belisarda, alarmed at the news of his inexplicable behavior, returns from Cyllene. Leonisa confirms her worst fears: Anfriso proclaims her unfaithful with Olimpio, has returned her love-tokens and given her old love-letters to Anarda in derision. On Anfriso's return, Frondoso vainly attempts to mediate. In a climactic scene, Belisarda and Anfriso, intent only upon wounding each other, flirt respectively with Olimpio and Anarda. The two women quarrel. Anfriso goes literally mad with jealousy, and has to be tied up. In a passion of despair, Belisarda marries her parents' choice. Galafrón and Frondoso take Anfriso to Polinesta, the wisest witch in Arcadia, who promises to heal him. Belisarda's wedding is celebrated with a great allegorical water-joust. Anfriso, convalescing of a "mortal melancholy," meets Belisarda accidentally by the fountain and they discover at last their mistake. But it is now too late. After a last mutual avowal of love, they part forever.

Book V: So far, the reader has been entertained. Now he is to be instructed, and shown that love can be cured, not by magic but by virtue and proper occupations. On their way to Polinesta, Anfriso and Frondoso visit the temple of Pan. Polinesta begins with a speech on the dangers of idleness followed by an interlude in which Cardenio comes to borrow the witch's *Book of Fortunes* for Isbella's party-games, and fortune-telling and palmistry are discussed. Then Anfriso, after a purification ceremony, is led through the Palace of the Liberal Arts (Grammar, Logic, Rhetoric, Arithmetic, Geometry, Music and Astronomy) and the *Palace of Poetry*. At the end, learning and poetry have put Belisarda quite out of his mind. He regrets the time wasted on love instead of pursuing eminence and fame, and sings the praises of the house of Alba. Finally, Polinesta leads him to the *Temple of Disillusionment*, where he sings the praises of that liberating experience. In an epilogue, *Belardo to his Rustic Flute*, the author bids farewell to pastoral. *Explanation of Historical and Poetical Names*: an appendix with Lope de Vega's own copious notes to the text of the novel.

III   *Biography, Autobiography, or Fiction?*

In *Arcadia*, the question whether the shepherds represent real-life characters is especially cogent because of Lope's own repeated assertions in the Prologue, elsewhere in the book, and in other writings, that his novel dealt with a true story. It is generally agreed that Anfriso represents Don Antonio, Duke of Alba, and the novel is part of a series of works of various kinds (as will be seen later) written around the Duke's life and loves. For the rest, however, no significant correspondence can be seen between the novel and the known facts of the Duke's life. The evidence has been brilliantly analyzed by Osuna.[2] His conclusion is that, of the main characters, only Anfriso is definitely identifiable, though there are several possible identifications among the subsidiary characters.

As for autobiographical content (suggested by Lope's indication that he had "wept over" his own misfortunes in writing about Anfriso's), though Lope is mentioned several times, as Belardo, he does not appear as one of the characters. Nor is a situation analogous to the Anfriso-Belarda-Olimpio-Anarda one detectable in his own life. But he *had* recently emerged from a period of emotional upheaval (his jealousy of Elena Osorio, the unfaithful mistress, his consequent wild behavior and banishment) and he *had* felt victimized and persecuted. *Arcadia* bears the stamp of these experiences. Jealousy and envy are main themes in the book. When Anfriso voices the pangs of separation, or thrashes about in agonies of jealousy and wounded self-esteem, there is little doubt that Lope is expressing feelings that are only too fresh in his own mind. But all this is far from adding up to anything that comes within range of autobiography. What we have is, in effect, an elaborate literary tribute to the Duke of Alba in the form of a work of fiction with a standard pastoral protagonist who looks like the nobleman, speaks sometimes with Lope's voice, but does not, in any real sense, stand for either.

IV   *Structure: Plot, Characters, and Ornamentation*

The qualities of *Arcadia* are not to be sought in its structure. Not that the minimum elements of a coherent structure are not present: a straightforward enough main plot (Anfriso/Belisarda) and a basic theme (disillusion), but they are submerged in the luxuriant growth of ornamental matter (descriptions, discussions, encyclopedic accounts, fables, entertainments, etc.) which makes up by far the largest proportion of the novel's not inconsiderable bulk.

The main plot on its own, including all directly relevant matter, would take up no more than the length of a short story or a play, and unlike the earlier major examples of the genre, there are no interacting parallel plots, nor subplots developed to any significant degree. The two rudimentary subplots represented by the Olimpio-Isbella and Anarda-Enareto relationships are strictly part of the mechanics of the main story. A third subplot is sketched in—that of mad Celio, unhinged by jealousy. This serves to introduce a display of insane behavior which prefigures Anfriso's own fit later on, and provides the excuse for one of the longer poems, the romance of Celio's love, as well as for a rhetorically polished prose lament by the sufferer himself. It serves no plot-related purpose, but demonstrates two characteristic aspects of Lope's technique: expansion by ornamentation, and the use of thematic elements.

An attempt to structure the development of the plot is made by the use of what might loosely be called a dramatic arrangement of the material.[3] That is to say that a number of key scenes are unfolded in detail before the reader, as if on a stage, and the remainder of the action, motivation, and necessary information is summarized in linking passages where Lope takes advantage of the novelist's privilege to impart information in condensed form by way of authorial explanation and comment. Ten such main "scenes" take the story from Belisarda's ill-omened dream and the first love scene to the lovers' last farewell. They are introduced by precise indications of setting and often also of time of day (in the manner of summary stage directions) and they are visualized and carried through in dramatic terms, with the unfolding of character and relationships taking place through speech and action.[4] This covers Books I to IV, Book V being in the nature of an epilogue in which the moral of the story is drawn.

The single plot focuses the attention on the central couple, who thus achieve more of the status of true protagonists. E. S. Morby (in his edition of the novel) has drawn attention to the unusual degree of care bestowed upon their character-drawing; and R. Osuna goes so far in his important study as to call Anfriso "the first modern character in the pastoral novel." [5] One need not, however, expect any considerable depth of psychological portrayal in the modern sense. Anfriso and Belisarda still operate on the whole at the same comparatively general level as the characters in other pastoral novels which is, however, not nearly as stereotyped as has often been claimed. As shown in earlier chapters, the Spanish pastoral novel showed from the beginning a greater concern with character and individuality than it has usually been credited with. In Lope de Vega, it is not so much a matter of finer psychological detail, but of a shift in the frame of reference. For all the insistence on the timeless world of pastoral (to the extent that it is the only Spanish pastoral novel set in the original lands of Arcadia), Lope's characters are very much like the townspeople and courtiers of his own time, whom he so often portrayed in his plays. These shepherds belong not with Montemayor's, but with such courtly, urban characters as Felismena and her volatile beau. Their frame of reference is not that of intemporal Neoplatonic paradigms, but of beings caught up in highly temporal dilemmas, hence the sense of greater actuality.

Anfriso is basically the type of the young protagonist of any number of contemporary plays or stories. In addition, he has one or two important individual features inherited from his creator: a taste for learning and an easily aroused jealousy. The latter is the characteristic on which the whole unhappy course of events hinges. It is the classic "tragic flaw" in an otherwise noble character and implies, with some psychological acuteness, his lack of confidence both in himself and in Belisarda: already at their first parting, and in spite of the proofs of utter devotion she has just given, he needs heavy reassurance from Silvio, who prophetically warns him: "nothing in this exile, *except your own thoughts*, can do you wrong; beware only of this enemy" (italics added).

Anfriso is as prone to jealousy as Othello, and he is his own most persuasive Iago. When he comes to spy on Belisarda, one feels that he does so for the sake of confirming, rather than dispelling, his obsession. From the moment when he has the flimsiest of apparent evidence to build on, he never looks back. He avoids explanations, refuses mediation, and seeks only to be revenged. Self-pity and the hurt to his own pride are foremost in his mind ("How can I, grievous me, beaten by my competitor, go on living among men?") yet when Belisarda retaliates in kind, he cannot take the strain. Overcome by his inner, self-created turmoil of love, jealousy, and hurt pride, he breaks down and has to be physically restrained. There follows Polinesta's treatment which is, in effect, a course of occupational therapy presented in allegorical style, in which she takes advantage of his other strong character trait, his taste for learning, to effect the entirely successful cure.

The unfortunate object of Anfriso's love is depicted sympathetically throughout. Lope is at pains to stress that her suffering is "unjust, and undeserved without a doubt." Her symbol is the white lamb of the sonnet she herself sings at one point, the lamb unjustly beaten by a jealous shepherd. She is carefully presented as a steady, sensible character, and emerges as one of the most balanced and likeable of pastoral heroines. Her wit is ready and her tongue can be sharp (as in her barbed exchange with Anarda) but there is no vanity or ill-nature in her. She is modest and unassuming in all her dealings—with her family, with Anfriso, and even with Olimpio, whose unwelcome and heavily pressed suit she rejects in reasonable, measured terms.

Reasonableness and good judgment are, in fact, her main character traits. She loves Anfriso not just for his obvious attractiveness, but for the real qualities of character that she detects in him. Her trust in him is complete. To suggest to her that he might be unfaithful is like asking her to believe that "sluggish oxen fly among the clouds." The greater is the shock, when it comes, of his unjust suspicions and brutal behavior. Wounded in her deepest feelings, mild, reasonable

Belisarda suddenly takes the most unreasonable step imaginable, and marries Salicio. As Lope comments: "harsh decree of a jealous woman . . . useless remedy and desperate purpose." The final parting neatly sums up the two main characters. He, as usual, is concerned above all with self-justification: he meant no harm, he says, and calls all imaginable punishments down on his own head "if I have offended you." She, true to the last, sings: "though my body is not my own/I leave my soul with you." She is fetched away by Salicio. He, with his friends, goes off to seek relief and forgetfulness.

The subsidiary characters are not many nor, with a few exceptions, more than summarily sketched in: Anfriso's old rivals Galafrón and Leriano, and Olimpio, the new one; Menalca, Isbella's new lover, valiant captain, and erudite storyteller; Anfriso's friends and confidants, Silvio and Frondoso; and Cardenio "the rustic," who deserves special mention: he plays a substantial role as a provider of both comic relief and deflating comment on the lovers' sentimental excesses, along the lines of the typical *gracioso* of Spanish Golden Age drama (a stock character combining clownishness with native wit and practical sense). The range of male characters is completed by a dozen or so personages with minor roles in the plot (Clorinardo— Belisarda's father, Alcino, Gaseno) or in thematic development (Celio's love madness), or those taking part in debates and performances (Benalcio the mathematician, Celso the epigrammatist, Danteo the sculptor, Brasildo the musician, and so on).

The number of individualized female characters is very small. This world of gallantry and sentiment, of course, revolves round them, but their role, except for the heroine herself, is a mainly passive one. They are the desirable prizes, and the admiring audiences, for the young men to whom action and the display of poetic and intellectual gifts are reserved. They emerge from anonymity only as strictly required for the plot: Isbella, the spirited coquette who transfers her favors from Olimpio to Menalca; Leonisa, the heroine's confidante; and, of course, Anarda, the innocent tool and incidental victim of Anfriso's revenge.

The most striking thing about *Arcadia* is perhaps the profusion of essentially ornamental matter. All pastoral novels have an element of decoration. What is unusual here is the inordinate importance given to such material and the tenuousness, in many cases, of its links with the action. No less than twenty-nine separate sections (in prose, in verse, or in a combination of the two) can be readily identified as being of this kind. Many of these fit into categories that are common enough in the pastoral genre: debates on love, literature, and related matters; inserted tales; descriptions of landscapes, temples, and palaces; games and entertainments; praises of patrons or famous personages. Others can be subsumed under the heading of Lope de Vega's characteristic fondness for imparting out-of-the-way information (such as Anfriso's speech on the secret properties of things, or Polinesta's *Book of Fortunes*). Some are quite brief (e.g., Cardenio's speech on the medicinal properties of donkeys), but others attain considerable proportions, and to all these must be added the 452 explanatory notes. In fact, well over half of *Arcadia* is made up of a mass of extraneous material, replete with heterogeneous and recondite allusions and references, whose primary purpose is to display erudition and literary skill in prose and in verse.

V   *The Pathology of Love and the Theme of Jealousy; Disillusionment; The Use of Magic; Learning and Literature*

In *Arcadia*, Lope de Vega reveals an insatiable appetite for facts and ideas, and an easy familiarity with the intellectual and artistic concerns of the age. The approach is entirely eclectic, not to say heterogeneous. Neoplatonism, the essential substratum of a pastoral novel, is naturally present, but it is implicit and diffuse, rather than formally elaborated. It is simply part of the atmosphere, an atmosphere which also comprises an admixture of Aristotelian ideas and terminology (such as the theory of the three souls: vegetative, appetitive, and rational) and large doses of the most miscellaneous information, adding up to a show of encyclopedic knowledge.

Avalle-Arce finds that "the philosophic-ideological attitude which most clearly emerges from the novel . . . is a Neo-Stoic one." [6] As long as it is clearly understood that Lope is not developing a Neo-Stoic theory in any formal sense, but simply displaying a certain attitude of mind, this is true enough, and takes us straight to the heart of the novel. In its attitude to love *Arcadia* is, in a sense, an anti-pastoral novel. Love is not accepted as a fate or an inclination with the glorious transcendent possibilities of Neoplatonic pastoral, but roundly condemned as a condition of suffering and madness, to be overcome by disillusionment and left behind on the way to other, worthier tasks. In his view of the matter, Lope de Vega is at variance with the Neoplatonists around him, echoing rather the medieval conception of love as a truancy to be repented, and foreshadowing the stern disenchantment with things of this world (well exemplified by

Quevedo) characteristic of Spanish writing in the seventeenth century.

It has been said that in *Arcadia*, "Lope describes the pathology of love, not its philosophy." [7] How true this is of its protagonist has already been seen in examining the character of Anfriso. His love is tainted with the sickness of jealousy. For Montemayor, jealousy was the hallmark of true love; for Gil Polo, the revealing blemish of bad love; Cervantes condemned it as a sign of lack of trust in one's beloved, and of confidence in oneself, and agreed with Gil Polo that it was, "like fever in a patient," a pathological symptom. But they both gave ample recognition to a true, healthy kind of love, of which jealous love was simply a form of corruption. Lope goes one step farther than all of them: he agrees with Gil Polo and Cervantes that jealousy is a disease, but he also agrees with Montemayor that it is inseparable from love; hence, *all* love is a disease. This is the disillusioned message of *Arcadia*. The fate of lovers is to suffer from jealousy and end in disappointment, if not madness and death, unless they have the strength to shed their illusions, follow good advice, and struggle through to the peace of a disillusioned view of existence. This, as has been seen, is exactly what Anfriso does. The conditions of his cure by Polinesta are worth examining. She stresses that there will be no resorting to "vain words and signs to do violence to your free will, which is impossible," and explains that love is born of idleness, and its best remedy is virtuous activity.

The interlude introduced at this point by Cardenio's arrival may seem a mere *divertissement*, but is in fact perfectly relevant. Cardenio arrives singing a robustly humorous parody of the usual lovers' complaint; fortune-telling is presented as no more than a party game, and Polinesta's demonstration of palmistry is dismissed by Cardenio who "said there was no other truth in such sciences than the will of heaven and the faults or virtues of men." In other words: lovers' complaints are absurd, and omens, fortune-telling, the influence of stars and other signs (so often appealed to by lovers) are things merely suitable for "games and entertainments." The only things that count are the will of Heaven and the moral responsibility of the individual. Treatment then takes place: purification, passage through the Palace of the Liberal Arts, and through the Palace of Poetry. The desired effect is achieved. Anfriso now condemns "an idle life, mad love and pressing desires" and "wishing to show what he had learned in passing through such celebrated schools" he performs the song in praise of the house of Alba. Thereupon he is judged ready to go forward to the point that marks the culmination of the whole process, the Temple of Disillusionment, where he will see the ex-votos of others who have won through to wisdom, and sing his own final disavowal of love and the praises of "holy disillusionment," that brings freedom and contentment.

The point is thoroughly driven home. In addition, Lope de Vega, speaking in his authorial capacity, reasserts it at appropriate moments, especially in the opening pages of the book, and again in introducing Book V as specifically devoted to pointing the moral. That was Lope de Vega's advice to his patron, and to his readers, no doubt earnestly meant at a time when the turbulence of his much-troubled love affair with Elena Osorio was still (in spite of the brief married domesticity he had meanwhile achieved with Isabel de Urbina) fresh in his mind. But it was advice which, in the light of his energetic love affairs for many decades to come, and right into his old age, he can hardly be said to have much heeded himself.

Very little need be said about Lope de Vega's use of magic. Of the two magicians, Polinesta—Anfriso's spiritual guide—does not resort to magic at all but (like Gil Polo's Felicia before her) to what we today call psychological techniques. This is consistent with the emphasis that Lope, like Gil Polo, places on the free will of the individual. Dardanio, on the other hand, lives up to expectations; he performs spells to call forth diabolic spirits, has them waft Anfriso and himself through the air, turns Anfriso into an old man and himself into a donkey in order to spy on Belisarda, and so on. The plot-related function of his intervention—to furnish the occasion for Anfriso's misunderstanding—could have been served just as well by any number of natural devices, and it is plain that Lope introduces this episode, reminiscent of the extravagant events common in romances of chivalry, simply as a piece of exciting entertainment and as an opportunity for the display of high-sounding writing (in the casting of the spell) and of learning (in the encyclopedic enumeration of the lands seen from the air).

The desire to make a display of erudition was strong in Lope de Vega. So was his genuine delight in factual information of all kinds. In addition to the copious notes of the *Explanation*, almost any page of *Arcadia* will yield a literary, historical, or mythological reference, a scientific or pseudoscientific fact, or a piece of recondite information, giving plenty of justification for the charge of pedantry often directed against it. And it is true enough that this constitutes today the main stumbling block for the modern reader. But the frequent editions of the novel in its own time, when it competed in popularity with Montemayor's *Diana* and left all others far behind, show that the contemporary public must have approved and enjoyed. Lope was not merely giving vent to a personal inclination but giving the public what it wanted, which was information of all kinds in easily assimilated form, as shown by the popularity of miscellanies and collections of maxims, anecdotes, and curious facts.[8]

In meeting this demand, Lope was also consciously acting out the Renaissance concept of the *poeta eruditus*, the poet as a repository of universal knowledge, to whom readers turned not only for entertainment, but also for instruction and edification.[9] "The poet not only has to know all sciences, or at least the principles of them all, but he has to have the greatest experience of things that happen on land and at sea . . . He must know exactly the behaviour, way of life and customs of all kinds of people and, finally, all the things that people talk about, deal with and live by, for there is nothing in the world so high or so very low that he may not have occasion to write about, from the Maker Himself to the lowest worm and monster on Earth." This passage illustrates the attitude perfectly. It is taken from the discussion on literature in Book III among the shepherds of Benalcio's learned group, in which the views of literature are expounded which Lope de Vega put into practice in *Arcadia*.

The model held up for general approval is a fable by Tirsi, "with elegant verses, and embellished with stories and moralities." This, of course, could be a description of *Arcadia* itself. As for the purpose of literature, "the business of the poet, said Benalcio, is truly to write in order to teach and to delight, . . . as the orator's purpose in speaking elegantly is to persuade, and the doctor's, to heal the disease." But it differs from other disciplines in the degree of achievement required. Elsewhere, a mediocre practitioner may be acceptable; in literature, it is excellence or nothing.[10] This is why it has been rightly said that poets must be inspired by some god, and they write in the heat of that inspiration.[11] But inspiration alone is not sufficient. Much learning is required, such as found in "the works of old Virgil, Homer and others, full of moral and natural philosophy, and full also of a thousand judicious remarks which show them to have been very great cosmographers and astrologers." And, as we have seen at the beginning of the passage, a vast range of experience must be added to knowledge of the sciences. What emerges is a reasonable enough view. To be a poet, three things are needed: inspiration (i.e. creative talent), knowledge, and experience of people and things.

After some discussion along Aristotelian lines of the different levels of literary style (high, subdivided into *tragic* or *heroic*; middle or *lyrical*; and low or *comic*), Lope touches upon one of the continuing concerns of sixteenth-century aesthetics and joins the great debate on the relative merits of nature and art. Benalcio declares that both elements are essential to true poetry. The writer needs both natural gifts *and* competence in the exercise of his craft. This is instantly qualified by Cardenio: in writing, for instance, a love poem, what you need is not so much artistic skill but natural, i.e. genuine feeling expressed simply and straightforwardly.[12] And he proceeds to make fun of the kind of show of learning of which Lope himself was only too fond. This is to some extent a piece of self-protective irony on the part of Lope, but it also expresses a genuine conviction which he largely exemplified in many of his plays.

Even in *Arcadia*, while indulging his taste for artifice, he does tend, when he stops to reflect, to give nature the primacy in the nature-versus-art contrast, as when Olimpio criticizes the stereotyped poetic presentation of female beauty.[13] Lope's considered view, however, is that propounded by Cardenio and recapitulated by Poetry herself in her Palace: "Although nature its harmony/at first instils with greater power/art brings its help, and vying with each other/they jointly reach such a degree of excellence/that seems like unto a rare and divine frenzy."[14] Although nature, by definition, comes first, it and art are complementary, not antagonistic, and creative achievement is the result of their interaction. It is interesting that Lope does not bring any large philosophical approach to bear on this question, but that he considers it strictly from the down-to-earth point of view of the practicing, professional writer. The seemingly "divine frenzy" of inspiration is, in fact, the combination of natural gifts and skilled craft.

VI   *Literary Form and Technique: Narrative and Description; Panegyrics, Prose, and Poetry*

On Lope de Vega's use of narrative, there is little to add to the discussion of the structure of *Arcadia*: the plot material is arranged in a series of key scenes enacted in the narrative present, linked by appropriate explanatory passages, and embedded in large quantities of ornamental matter, of which the most substantial proportion is composed of descriptions. The descriptive elements are of various kinds, ranging from major set-pieces, such as the description of Arcadia, or of the Temple of Pan, to references to setting, physical appearance and clothing of characters, etc., interspersed in narrative passages.

The set-pieces are ambitious constructions designed to display to best advantage the author's literary skills, command of language, range of learned allusion, and knowledge of a great variety of subjects. The opening of the novel is a characteristic example of Lope de Vega's technique. The description of the geographical location and main topographical features of Mount Menalus and its valley, in the heart of the Peloponnesus, is followed by an extended account of the local flora, the purpose of which is not only descriptive or botanical. The mention of virtually each flower or plant is accompanied by a mythological or literary allusion and often by a reference to its supposed special properties (e.g., "the red rose, which restored Apuleius to his former shape, born of the blood of Venus's feet when she rushed through the thorns to rescue Adonis and the flower into which he was transformed by her . . ."; or "blond hyacinths, from which scorpions take flight"). The interaction of literary and mythological allusions is, however, not merely a matter of ornamental display. It also signals to the reader at once the learned, literary character of the work being placed before him. This is no straightforward description, but—in Osuna's apt phrase—an interpretation of the Arcadian landscape,[15] starting on its way a work in which setting, characters, and action will all be seen through the prism of literature. The image of the prism, which creates a glittering, vivid, many-colored world, is significantly used by Lope in this same passage: "for not otherwise did the merry fields look as when one places triangular glasses before one's eyes, whereby all things one gazes on appear in changing colors and iridescent hues."

A few words need to be said about the panegyric aspect of *Arcadia*. In Montemayor and Gil Polo, the laudatory poems remain pure accretions. Cervantes connects up his praise of writers somewhat more firmly through the device of the funeral rites, but Calliope's song is still extraneous to the business of the novel. *Arcadia*, on the other hand, was conceived as a tribute to the patron at whose court it was written, and the element of praise is woven into the fabric of the novel itself, operating at several levels.

To begin with, as Anfriso stands for the Duke Don Antonio, the frequent laudatory remarks about his birth, handsomeness, wit or other qualities, are direct compliments to the patron. So is the elegiac sonnet, praising in grandiloquent terms the qualities of Anfriso's (Don Antonio's) deceased mother. And the progress of the protagonist from amorous folly to the pursuit of nobler aims, implying a similar capacity for self-fulfillment in Don Antonio, is a further kind of compliment. But the highest flattery is that of juxtaposing Don Antonio with the figure of his truly distinguished grandfather, Don Fernando Alvarez de Toledo (1507–1582), the leading general of Charles V and Philip II. Don Fernando's praises are sung on several occasions: in the sonnet on one of the empty sepulchres in Book II, in the praise of heroes in Dardanio's cave, and most extensively in the poem in praise of the house of Alba where it is prophesied that Don Antonio will prove his worthy successor. The placing of this paean of praise in Anfriso's mouth involves a curious splitting of the protagonist's personality. Anfriso, who has ostensibly been a "mask" for Don Antonio all along, now stands aside from himself, as it were, and sings the praises of the Duke, which illustrates the extent to which the main character in the novel is, in fact, a combination of patron and author. At this closing stage, the author takes over entirely, and Anfriso becomes simply his mouthpiece.

All this would seem to be quite enough panegyric for one pastoral novel. But Lope de Vega, the "prodigy of nature," tends to excess in everything. He wants to run the gamut of usual laudatory exercises. Hence the gallery of heroes, praised in prose and in verse, in Dardanio's cave, and the passage in praise of poets in the Palace of Poetry. Finally, the sonnets in Book II to the Marquess of Santa Cruz (a famous admiral under whom Lope had served) and to Don Gonzalo Girón (ancestor of the Duke of Osuna, to whom *Arcadia* was dedicated on publication) complete the range of laudatory material.

Lope de Vega's prose style in *Arcadia* is consistent with the general character of the book, rich, courtly, and elaborate. The ornamental nature of much of the material is matched in presentation by a similar taste for decorative writing, characterized by the use of an abundant, highly varied terminology drawn from many different fields. The syntax can be quite straightforward in passages (such as the description of the Temple of Pales) that rely for their effect on the accumulation of individually simple elements. Elsewhere, the prose syntax of *Arcadia* is in keeping with the overall tendency toward elaboration.

The opening sentence of the novel is a good example of this. The basic statement about the location of Mount Menalus between two rivers is expanded, by means of subordinate clauses and subordinates of subordinates, and by a profusion of epithets (every noun has at least one) to cover fourteen lines in one continuous sentence.

Narrative passages and the shepherds' speeches (e.g., Anfriso's first greeting to Belisarda) are mostly in a similarly complex mode, using a kind of language which, alien though it may sound to a modern sensibility, was much to the taste of contemporary readers. In some ways it was a continuation and development of the pursuit of rhetorical elegance in late medieval sentimental novels such as those of Diego de San Pedro.[16] But in those works of an earlier age a firmly controlled balance was attempted, and largely achieved. Closer precedents to the language of *Arcadia* are to be found in the romances of chivalry which had been so immensely popular in the first half of the sixteenth century, and whose tendency to bombast and to inextricable syntax was soon to achieve burlesque immortality by turning Don Quixote's brain.

In sharp contrast, the first pastoral novelists, Montemayor and Gil Polo, had used a type of prose that aimed at simplicity, suppleness, and directness of effect. But as the sixteenth century drew to its close, the taste for a complex, high-sounding diction was reasserting itself. It was to reach its full flower in the seventeenth-century style of *culteranismo*: syntactically involved, richly-wrought, and endlessly allusive.[17] In the first decades of that century, Lope de Vega was one of the most bitingly vocal of eminent men who launched attacks upon it. Yet *Arcadia* shows to what extent, back in the 1580s and 1590s, he had accurately gauged the taste of the new reading public and quietly done his best to cater to it.

Both the prose and the poetry of *Arcadia* are moved by a similar desire to demonstrate high achievement through richness and elaboration, but in the latter Lope de Vega was much more in his element. His lyrical poetic gifts were of the highest order, and his facility as a versifier phenomenal. Although this last fact could sometimes result in superficiality or hasty finish, what is most striking in his enormous verse production is the cogency of poetic statement and the prevailing high level of sheer craftsmanship.[18] *Arcadia* is a fair example of this. In it, Lope took advantage of the genre's traditional blending of prose and verse to introduce a very large number of poems. In fact, a rough calculation shows that the novel contains more lines of verse—some six thousand in all—than of prose.[19]

The range of forms includes most of the usual ones. Lope de Vega was equally at home in both traditional Spanish and Italianate verse. In the former, his handling of the folk-ballad *romance* which had hardly been used in pastoral novels before him is especially noteworthy. The four such ballads in *Arcadia* are all highly successful, in particular Alasto's song to Crisalda "Cuando sale el alba hermosa" ("When beautiful dawn breaks") and the story of Celio's unhappy love, "En las riberas famosas" ("On the famous banks"), two of the best poems in the whole book.

As regards Italianate forms, one may note particularly the sonnet and the *canción*. Lope was one of the most accomplished sonneteers of his time, and *Arcadia* is studded with numerous examples of the form (twenty-four in all). A good proportion of these are remarkable for their quality, especially Belisarda's gentle and prophetic "Silvio a una blanca corderilla suya" ("Silvio to his little white lamb")—probably the best-known poem in the whole *Arcadia*—and, in a lighter vein, Celso's sonnet to his beloved's comb "Por las ondas del mar de unos cabellos" ("Through the waves of a sea of hair"). *Canciones* are also frequent and are the subject of a good deal of structural experimentation falling into no less than eleven different categories out of a total of fourteen compositions, with variations in meter, rhyme patterns, numbers of verses per stanza, and so on.

The materials and techniques of Lope's poetry are largely those of the Petrarchan tradition. This is one of the main roots of his poetic style, the others being a continuous taste for the antitheses and conceits of the Spanish tradition of courtly lyrics, and his own particularly close relationship with the themes, styles, and forms of folk-poetry. He was especially fond of the characteristic Petrarchan technique of "correlation" and "multiple enumeration" (which we have already mentioned in connection with Cervantes), and became well-known to his contemporaries as a master in its utilization. So much so that a literary theorist, Jiménez Patón, in his treatise *Eloquencia Española* (1604), published only six years after *Arcadia*, took him as the leading authority in the use of this poetic technique, and *Arcadia* as the best source of quotations to illustrate its various forms.[20] The verses are undoubtedly the most successful part of *Arcadia*. Thanks to the discipline of prosody, Lope de Vega's inexhaustible flow of vocabulary, imagery, word play and thought play is cast into definite, highly polished forms. The comparison with precious objects comes to mind, fashioned from rich materials with superb craftsmanship.

VII   *Literary Sources*

In the choice of title, as well as in the opening and closing scenes (which echo the *locus amoenus* with which Sannazaro started *Arcadia*, and the farewell to Sincero's flute with which he closed it), Lope de Vega explicitly related his own *Arcadia* to the Neapolitan's novel. Apart from this, however, the traces of Sannazaro are general, rather than specific, in character.[21] There is little, in fact, that Lope owes to any particular model as regards structure or plot. On the other hand, he copiously wove into the texture of the novel, by way of reference, quotation, imitation, or straight translation, specific literary materials from a wide range of sources.

In fellow Spaniards, Lope found a number of ideas: Anfriso's and Belisarda's partings, for instance, may have been suggested by Montemayor; the water joust has a clear precedent in Gil Polo's; the performance on an eclogue is found for the first time in Gálvez de Montalvo's *El Pastor de Filida* (see Ch. 6), and again in Cervantes' *Galatea*; Anfriso reading an old love letter when exiled from Belisarda recalls Sireno reading Diana's at the beginning of Montemayor's novel. These are all, however, of a fairly general nature, and direct quotations or imitations of Spanish materials are rare.

From Italy, besides the whole tradition of Petrarchan poetry, Ariosto's great poem, the *Orlando furioso* (1516), should be noted as a source of particular relevance to the theme of jealous madness: Celio's and Anfriso's behavior during their outbursts follows the pattern set by Ariosto in the famous scene of Orlando's madness in Canto XXIII. In Anfriso's case, the connection is explicit: "like another Orlando, he was tearing branches off the trees." This was a theme to which Lope often returned and which was to furnish the basis of at least two entire works of his: the epic poem *La hermosura de Angélica* (The Beauty of Angelica) (1602), and the play *Belardo el furioso* (Belardo in his Frenzy). In *Arcadia* it crops up again in the water joust where the figures of Orlando, Angélica, and Medoro decorate Galafrón's boat.

Classical reminiscences are abundant, and frequently specific. There are imitations and adaptation from Horace (including not only the usual *Beatus ille*, but also less well known materials from other Odes), translations from Propertius, Catullus, and Ausonius, prose paraphrases of Tibullus and Catullus; the examples could be multiplied. The presence of Ovid, for centuries the main source of love advice (*Ars Amatoria*) and of mythological lore (*Metamorphoses*) is, as

might be expected, pervasive. Mythological allusions are innumer-
able and it is Ovid who informs the two mythological fables: *Alasto
and Crisalda* (a variant of the Polyphemus-Galatea story) and *Jupiter,
the Rose, and the Snake* (freely constructed after the pattern of an
Ovidian metamorphosis). Finally, Virgil is present more by implication, as the fountainhead, with Theocritus, of the pastoral tradition
altogether and mediately through the example of Sannazaro. The
dusk scene toward the end of Book II, however, includes a close
translation of the Virgilian original.

In addition to the elements of literary tradition which he handled
with easy spontaneity, Lope de Vega also sought to satisfy his and his
readers' taste for encyclopedic learning by extracting large quantities
of varied and unusual information and materials from compendia and
books of miscellanies of the type that had been extremely popular
from the fifteenth century onward.[22] Several of these have been
identified, including: Joannes Ravisius Textor's vast *Officina* (from
which many of the references in the initial description of the Arcadian
lands are taken), Frans Titelmans' *Compendium*, dealing especially
with cosmological and psychological concepts, and Constantino Cas-
triota's *Il sapere utile e delettevole*, a mine of information on natural
history and the alleged properties of plants, animals, and stones. Two
substantial sections in Book V (the *Book of Fortunes* and the *Palace of
the Liberal Arts*) depend entirely on one particular authority each.
The former is based on Lorenzo Spirito's *Delle Sorti*, one of the most
popular books of this kind. The latter has been qualified, not unfairly,
as downright plagiarism. Everything in Lope's *Palace of the Liberal
Arts* is taken straight from a fifteenth-century allegorical treatise,
Alfonso de la Torre's *Visión deleitable de la filosofia y de otras
ciencias* (Delectable Vision of Philosophy and other Sciences) which
had enjoyed a considerable success for over a century, to the extent of
being translated into Italian in 1556.[23] Finally, the vast *Explanation
of Historical and Poetical Names*, the culmination of Lope's display of
erudition, is based to a large extent, often verbatim, on a contemporary encyclopedia, Carolus Stephanus' *Dictionarium historicum,
geographicum, poeticum*.

VIII   *Lope de Vega and the Pastoral Mode*

It is curious that, while pastoral poetry kept flowing freely from
poets' pens, pastoral in the form of a novel seems to have exhausted
itself, for each author, in one single effort. Even Cervantes, who

clung to the last to the thought of a sequel to *Galatea*, never managed to turn wish into reality. Lope de Vega, for all his verve and facility in other genres, was no exception. *Arcadia* is his only true pastoral novel. But, for him as for Cervantes the pastoral mode remained a lifelong attraction. He wrote several pastoral plays, the last, *Selva sin Amor* (*Forest without Love*), as late as 1629, when he was sixty-seven. He also wrote love lyrics cast in the pastoral mold, which crop up at many points in his dramatic and other works. Lope's lyric use of the verse eclogue, however, went beyond the usual range of love poetry. In his declining years, after 1632, he turned to it for the expression of deeply felt personal sorrow in the three great eclogues *Amarilis, Felicio,* and *Filis*.[24]

Pastoral was also considered an eminently suitable vehicle for laudatory verse, to sing of the loves or celebrate the successes of the great, and we have seen that the whole of *Arcadia* is, at one level, a panegyric exercise. The figure of Don Antonio, the Duke of Alba, inspired a number of other works which have in common not only the person of the Duke, but also many of the elements of literary elaboration to which it was subjected. This series of works, interrelated to varying degrees, but all having in common the figure of the protagonist and the treatment in pastoral mode, has been appropriately described as the "Duke of Alba cycle." [25] It includes, in addition to *Arcadia* itself, three pastoral plays: *La pastoral de Jacinto, Los amores de Albanio y Ismenia* and *La Arcadia*; one eclogue, *Egloga primera al Duque de Alba*; one descriptive poem, *La descripción de "La Abadfa," jardín del Duque de Alba*, and about a dozen pastoral *romances*. In time, these works range from about 1591 (when Lope came into the service of Don Antonio) to about 1615 (probable date of the play *La Arcadia*). Thematically, the novel *Arcadia* occupies the central point in this cycle, bringing together and exploring at greater length all the various sentimental, ideological, and literary strands that run through the different works.

Finally, it should be noted that Lope de Vega also made a substantial contribution to the tradition of religious pastoral. His collection of *Rimas sacras* (published 1614) contains sonnets and other compositions in which pastoral terminology and images are put to devotional uses. He also wrote a full-size religious pastoral novel, *The Shepherds of Bethlehem*, which we shall discuss in the next chapter.

CHAPTER 6

The Other Pastoral Novels: A Conspectus

I N the preceding chapters, four major Spanish pastoral novels have
been examined in some detail. To complete the picture, we must
now turn to the other examples of the genre, some twenty in all,
written mainly over the three-quarters of a century during which it
flourished from the late 1550s onward. To give each one of these a
similarly close treatment is neither possible nor necessary within the
scope of the present volume. Apart from the often-quoted works by
Rennert and Avalle-Arce,[1] very little attention has so far been paid to
these novels: studies in depth are lacking in all cases, and there are
very few modern editions of the texts. Those that do exist are not
recent, and are difficult to obtain.[2] Part I of the present chapter is
therefore designed primarily as a brief conspectus of all the works
which can be regarded as falling within the category, arranged chron-
ologically. Part II briefly surveys the handful of pastoral novels in
so-called *"a lo divino"* (i.e., religious-allegorical) versions to which
the vogue of the genre gave rise. Part III lists some marginal works.

I   The Other Pastoral Novels

1 *Alonso Pérez: Segunda Parte de la Diana de George de Montemayor* (Second Part of the Diana of George de Montemayor)
Valencia, 1563.

As with many others of the minor pastoral authors, hardly anything
is known about the writer's personality. He seems to have been a
physician of Salamanca and no other works from his pen are known.
He may be the same Dr. Alonso Pérez who taught natural philosophy
at Salamanca University, wrote two learned treatises in Latin, and
died in 1596. Pérez's *Second Part* was the first attempt to ride the

wave of the original *Diana's* popularity by writing the sequel that
Montemayor had announced but failed to produce. (It was closely
followed, within the year, by Gil Polo's, vastly superior as literature,
and many years later by Tejeda's unscrupulous effort—see no. 17
below).

Pérez takes over Montemayor's main characters and adds a number of his own, such as Firmio and Fausto, Diana's new suitors, and
Parisiles, the "most worthy priest of Jupiter," who joins Felicia as a
dispenser of wisdom. Diana's husband Delio dies, and the novel ends
with the announcement of a *Third Part* which was, again, never
written. The inset tale of Partenio and Delicio, whose characters
interact with the main plot at several points, remains unresolved.
Another insertion is the long poem narrating the mythological tale of
Daphne and Apollo.

As continuator of the first *Diana*, Alonso Pérez claimed an author-
itative position: Montemayor (he wrote in his introduction) had discussed with him plans for a sequel before he left Spain on his last
journey. And he regarded himself not only as a worthy successor, but
as in many ways a better qualified one. While praising Montemayor's
facility and the qualities of his verse and prose, he deplored his lack of
classical culture. By way of contrast, Pérez proudly claimed for
himself a thorough exercise of *imitatio*, in the best classical tradition:
"In the whole of this work there is hardly a narrative or conversation,
not only in verse, but even more so in prose, which is not purloined
and imitated in pieces from the flower of Latins and Italians, nor do I
think that I should be rebuked on that account, since they did the
same with the Greeks." The overall connection with Sannazaro is
clear but, apart from a couple of passages derived from his *Arcadia*,
there do not seem to be any very concrete imitations of Italian
models. The influence of classical Latin literature, on the other hand,
is ubiquitous, in the form of allusions, references, and paraphrases
rather than direct quotations, and most particularly in the wealth of
mythological material.

Pérez, following the general example of Sannazaro, was intent
upon combining elements from many sources into a mosaic-like
pattern. A good instance of this is the story of Partenio and Delicio,
which combines the traditional tale of the "two friends" with the
theme of the comedy of errors resulting from the activities of identical
twins, and grafts onto this, in the Gorforoso-Stela subplot, the motif
of Polyphemus' pursuit of the nymph Galatea. Furthermore, the tale
is related, through the story of the twins' royal parents, to the world of

the romances of chivalry. For all the superficial connections with the plot and characters of the first *Diana*, the endeavor to compose a literary artifact consciously (one might say, self-consciously) linked to the mainstream of a humanistic cultural tradition places Pérez's novel closer in nature and in literary intent to Sannazaro's exquisitely learned *Arcadia* than to Montemayor's exercise in sentimental analysis.

In his conception of love, Pérez turns away from the Neoplatonic views which informed the thought and sensibility of his models. His philosophy is colored by the tradition of Christian Scholasticism, reinvigorated at that time by the rising tide of the Counter-Reformation (the Council of Trent closed its long-drawn-out debates in the same year that the second *Diana* was published). Human love is seen as a dangerous desire, immoderate in its impulses and all too often changeable in its pursuit of satisfaction. It is not an ennobling or potentially ennobling experience, but a disease of the soul.

As a writer, Alonso Pérez lacked the literary gifts of both his models, and failed to achieve any kind of synthesis of the varied elements he brought together. His sense of structure is deficient, his prose overelaborate, his poetry prosy. Yet the number of editions of his *Diana* published well into the seventeenth century seems to indicate that it filled an obvious need. The bare figures, however, can be deceptive. To a large extent, what happened was that Pérez was swept along in the wake of Montemayor's popularity. Ten of the seventeen Spanish editions did not appear independently, but appended to the first *Diana*, as its "*Second Part.*" The same situation obtained in the case of the translations; volumes were frequently issued comprising two or three "Parts of the *Diana* of Montemayor," i.e., Montemayor's own, Alonso Pérez's as Second, and, sometimes Gil Polo's as Third.

2 *Antonio de Lofrasso: Los Diez Libros de la Fortuna de Amor* (Ten Books of The Fortune of Love). Barcelona, 1573.

The author was a native of the Catalan-speaking city of L'Alguer (modern Alghero) in Sardinia (which had been under the Crown of Aragon since 1409), and a soldier by profession. His only other extant work is a *Letter from the Author to his Sons* (1571).

The ten books of *The Fortune of Love* fall naturally into three sections: Books I to V, set in Sardinia, comprise the pastoral novel proper; Books VI to IX are set in Barcelona, and the action is entirely urban, courtly, and documentary rather than fictional; finally, Book X, separately entitled *Garden of Love, of Various Rhymes*, is simply an appended collection of Lofrasso's verse, bearing no relation to the remainder of the work. The pastoral section of Lofrasso's work includes most of the elements typical of the genre, but the ideal pastoral world is here firmly rooted in the real landscape and geography of Sardinia, to a much greater extent than Montemayor's was in the valley of the Ezla, or Gil Polo's in Valencia. Frexano, the protagonist, is shown wooing his shepherdess Fortuna, suffering the pangs of unrequited love, giving vent to his feelings in song, and engaging in debate with other pastoral characters. He makes an allegorical journey to Parnassus, where he meets Minerva and the nine Muses. He is also involved in more adventurous situations, such as we have seen in Gil Polo and Cervantes, involving pirate attacks and storms at sea, which illustrate the frequent appearance in pastoral novels of plot devices borrowed from the Greek romances.

Other elements are derived from medieval literary tradition: the figure of wisdom is here Dame Belidea. Though her name (*Bella Idea*) has a Neoplatonic ring, there is little of the Renaissance about her: she presides over a typically medieval Court of Love, where "questions of love" are subjected to the kind of debate that goes back to twelfth century *cours d'amour*, rather than to the philosophical approach of a Leone Ebreo or a Bembo. There is also some use of medieval allegory (the visit to the Palace of Discontent of Love), and of the "rustic" type of shepherd familiar from Encina's or Lucas Fernández's plays (in a game of cow-baiting). The inevitable panegyric takes the form of a poem in praise of the ladies of L'Alguer. The claim that autobiographical material is being presented under pastoral guise is both made explicitly and implied in the protagonist's choice of name, Frexano being obviously derived from *fraxinus* (the ash tree; significantly, one of the most frequently mentioned species in pastoral landscapes since Virgil), of which Lofrasso is an Italianized form. The name of Frexano's shepherdess may also be intended as an allegorical hint; the writer and the soldier both woo Fortune.

Frexano's pastoral existence in Sardinia comes to an end when he is seized as suspect in a murder case. Upon his release he travels to Barcelona and enters the service of a noble family. Books VI to IX are devoted to a description of the life of courtly circles in Barcelona— festivals, entertainments, weddings, jousts, balls—and includes a description of the city and a poem praising the beauty of its ladies, a long *History of Don Floricio and the Beautiful Shepherdess Argenti-*

na (in which the only pastoral thing is the description of the lady as a "shepherdess"), and the detailed account of a royal tournament. The proportion of poetry to prose is very high throughout the book, including not only the bulk of Castilian verse, but also compositions in Catalan and in Sardinian. Unfortunately, neither prose nor verse is particularly memorable in quality. In the history of the Spanish pastoral novel, *The Fortune of Love* is mainly remarkable as an example of eclecticism. A soldier with a certain facility for writing, Lofrasso ranges far and wide, drawing upon his varied experience of life and a broad rather than scholarly knowledge of literature. Coming only some fifteen years after the beginnings of the genre, Lofrasso's novel already displays two characteristics that led to its decay: the proliferation of disparate materials (which, though with redeeming factors, reached a peak with Lope de Vega's encyclopedic *Arcadia*) and, rather more importantly, the tendency for the pastoral element to dwindle to a superficial convention. In this connection, it is significant that, in spite of its title, no reasoned consideration of love or any thought about the subject which goes beyond the current commonplaces is apparent in this novel. Still, the author knew well enough that some show of love philosophizing was expected. So, he duly produced a discussion on love, by and large Neoplatonic in drift, inserting it, not in the pastoral section of the book, but among the pastimes of Barcelona high society in the latter part. This separation is unwittingly symbolic. The pastoral world of the Renaissance had been born of the earnest aspirations of humanists and philosophically inclined courtiers. As it lost its ideal potency, the Neoplatonic thinking which had infused it with its peculiar radiance returned to the courtly circles whence it had sprung, but reduced to the status of a parlor game.

3. Luis Galvez de Montalvo: El Pastor de Filida (The Shepherd of Filida) Madrid, 1582.

Gálvez de Montalvo (Guadalajara? 1549–Sicily? 1591), "gentleman-at-court," as he made a point of stressing in his title page, enjoyed a literary reputation in his time (earning praise from both Cervantes and Lope de Vega), but his only other extant work is a translation into Spanish (published 1587) of Luigi Tansilo's poem *Le lagrime di San Pietro* (1585). In *The Shepherd of Filida* (as in Lope de Vega's *Arcadia* some sixteen years later), the patron for whom it was written and his entourage as well as the writer himself are substantially involved in the fabric of the book. Although the proportion of biographical or autobiographical material is hard to determine, the two leading shepherds, Mendino and Siralvo, stand respectively for Don Enrique de Mendoza y Aragón (at one level, the book is conceived as a panegyric to the house of Mendoza), and for Gálvez de Montalvo himself. The other shepherds include several noblemen and patrons of the arts, and poets, musicians, and artists who moved in the same artistic circles as Gálvez de Montalvo and his friend Cervantes. Some of them, most notably Tirsi (Francisco de Figueroa), reappeared three years later in *Galatea*.

Part I (of the seven which compose the novel) is devoted to Mendino's love affair with Elisa. This runs a happy course for three years before being tragically brought to an end by her illness and death. After the funeral games, reminiscent of those in Sannazaro, the focus of interest shifts to Siralvo's (the poet's) love for Filida, and her sympathetic acceptance of his chastely undemanding homage. To foil her family's intentions to force her into an unwanted marriage, she "devotes herself to chaste Diana" and becomes one of her nymphs; in nonpastoral language, she enters a convent. A solution unique in pastoral novels, this places the relationship on a permanently platonic basis, acceptable enough to Siralvo, who had already declared that "I do not ask Filida to love me, but that I live in the utmost contentment as long as she is not displeased with my loving her." [4] Several subsidiary love stories—Orindo and Finea, Arsiano and Silvera, Alfeo and Andria—are happily resolved thanks to Siralvo's mediation.

There is very little theorizing about love. The underlying attitude does not owe much, if anything, to Neoplatonic ideology, but rather harks back to the medieval conception of a love service which is its own reward. Siralvo's love for Filida is not the first step in a possible dynamic process of spiritual refinement, but the static adoration of an object regarded as quasi-divine in herself. It is as significant that, in entering the service of Diana, Filida becomes a nymph, a semi-divine being, and is referred to thereafter as a "mountain goddess."

The striking feature of *the Shepherd of Filida* is its exclusion of adventure or intrigue to concentrate on the pastoral world. Only two outside characters are brought in, Alfeo, a gentleman from Mantua, and his lady love. They are not, however, made the occasion for an inset story. On his first appearance, Alfeo merely sketches in the nonpastoral background, and thereafter their relationship works itself out on the pastoral plane, which they leave at the end to return to their normal town life. The descriptive and ornamental passages (including magicians' caves, and temples of Pan and of Diana) are generally brief, and fit economically into the overall development of the story. There are only three digressions of any importance: the performance of a verse *Eclogue*, a poem in praise of noble ladies, and a literary debate in which the respective merits of Italianate and traditional Spanish poetry are weighed and the judgment, though nicely balanced, comes down in favor of the latter because "our language is best suited by its own kind [of verse]."

Gálvez de Montalvo's literary practice is largely in accordance with his theory. He is a not inconsiderable poet in both types of verse, but his more felicitous efforts are mainly couched in traditional Spanish forms. In his prose, he follows to a remarkable extent his own recommendation of "plainness and sobriety" without eschewing, however, richer textures at some points. Bucolic events, natural settings, shifting sentimental relationships, and expressions of lovers' feelings are skillfully combined into a gentle, unhurried flow which is by no means devoid of interest and offers a good deal of aesthetic satisfaction. It also produces a more consistent pastoral picture than many other novels of the kind managed or even attempted. There is, however, an important difference between this pastoral world and that of Montemayor and Gil Polo or the efforts, still to come, of Cervantes and Lope de Vega. In their different ways, those authors use the pastoral mode to make some kind of statement about the nature of love and the nature of man, which reaches out to fundamentals. Gálvez de Montalvo, on the other hand, does not attempt to delve below the surface of events. The pastoral vision becomes here a matter of anecdote, setting, and expressive idiom. He deals with the particular—specific love affairs as they actually occurred around him—not with the general.

Gálvez de Montalvo was well aware of the fact that a pastoral that reflected more closely the events and fabric of actual society tended thereby to invite comparison with the circumstances of everyday existence and thus became less, rather than more, credible than one that relied entirely on purely ideal standards. Hence his mock-apologetic passage at the beginning of Part VI. He suggests that more or less far-fetched "realistic" justifications can always be found (e.g., sheepowners have time for love and songs because they employ ordinary shepherds and shepherd's boys to do their work for them) but good-humoredly discards them. He is not going to seek such justifications, but carry on with the story: "Thus might I well answer whatever charges might be brought against me; but since I refrain from doing so, there will surely be no lack of some kindly and discerning person to defend me in my absence if need be. Trusting in which I now proceed . . . ."

4 *Luis Hurtado de Toledo: El Teatro Pastoril en la Ribera de Tajo* (Pastoral Theatre on the Banks of the Tagus)

This unpublished manuscript, dated 1582, cannot have been read beyond a restricted circle, and remained thus outside the mainstream of the Spanish literature of the time.[5] Although it clearly belongs in a survey of pastoral novels, nothing beyond a bibliographical note can be given until such time as it becomes available in a scholarly edition. Its author, Luis Hurtado de Toledo (c. 1510–c. 1598) was a parish priest with a literary bent who became involved in producing editions of various texts not his own, including one of the most famous romances of chivalry, *Palmerín de Inglaterra* (1547), whose authorship was at one time attributed to him. He also wrote various works in verse and in prose, including some pastoral poetry, and the *Teatro pastoril*, a prose pastoral with some inserted verse which qualifies as a small pastoral novel.

Two earlier works by Hurtado de Toledo may be numbered among the forerunners of the pastoral novel in verse and in prose. They are the *Egloga silviana del galardón de amor* (*Sylvian Eclogue of the Prize of Love*), and the *Cortes de Casto Amor* (*Parliament of Chaste Love*), published respectively in 1553 and 1557. The former is a dramatic eclogue in verse. The latter is a short allegorical novel (praising chaste human love as leading to divine love) but includes, in setting and treatment, some of the typical elements of a pastoral novel.

5 *Bartolome López de Enciso: Desengaño de Celos* (Disillusionment of Jealousy) Madrid, 1586.

According to the title page, the author was a "native of Tendilla" (a small town in the province of Guadalajara). In fulfillment of the cautionary purpose advertised in the title, and explicitly stressed in the introductory *Epistle*, the six *Books* that compose the novel display abundant examples of the ravages of jealousy among the shepherds. There are inset stories which, apart from constituting further evidence of the insanity of jealousy and the sufferings of love generally, do not mesh in any way with the main structure, but remain tales told as separate entities.

The striking characteristic of *Disillusionment of Jealousy*, otherwise constructed with standard elements, is its strongly moralizing tone, which reminds one of Gil Polo's strictures on jealousy as the mark of evil love. In fact, López de Enciso's ideology has much in common with that of his predecessor. But where Gil Polo stresses the reasonable nature of true love, and its positive fulfillment, López de Enciso is intensely concerned with the condemnation of jealousy as irrational, and proceeds from that to the consideration of ethical problems on the basis of the exercise of free will under the supreme guidance of reason. We saw in Gil Polo the element of Stoic philosophy which this approach involves. This is much more marked in López de Enciso, to the extent that one of his shepherdesses has recourse to the ultimate Stoic affirmation of individual freedom: when faced with an insoluble dilemma, she commits suicide, a radical solution which is quite exceptional in the pastoral novel, apart from being highly likely to attract the unfavorable attention of the ecclesiastical authorities. Lovelorn shepherds occasionally die of a broken heart, and all too often express the wish to do so, but they do not actually take their own lives. Even Cervantes, whose range is so much wider than that of the other writers of pastoral, skirts the issue: in *Galatea*, Galercio's attempt to drown himself is foiled, and "defused" by being given a quasi-burlesque treatment. And in the pastoral episode of Grisóstomo and Marcela in *Don Quixote* the possibility of suicide is only hinted at with careful ambiguity.

In spite of its first appearing at a time when the vogue of pastoral was in full swing, *Disillusionment of Jealousy* was never reprinted. Its stern attitude must have discouraged readers. In any case, it did not have much to recommend it by way of literary worth. The verse achieves pleasingly euphonious effects, but neither the quality of the prose nor the handling of plot and incident rise above a modest mediocrity.

6 *Bernardo González de Bobadilla: Primera Parte de las Ninfas y los Pastores de Henares* (First Part of the Nymphs and Shepherds of the Henares) Alcalá, 1587.

Very little need be said about this. It is the work of a young man (a native of the Canary Islands, and a student at Salamanca University), written with more enthusiasm than literary skill. It comprises all the usual components of pastoral novels, plus a good deal of violent action—kidnappings, woundings, and deaths. There are a few Neoplatonic statements about love, just as a matter of form but, for all the conventional surface protestations, love is here a matter that definitely requires sensual satisfaction. Lisia the shepherdess, for instance, admits her lover into her bedroom every night.

The most unusual thing about *The Nymphs and Shepherds of the Henares* is undoubtedly the reason given by the author for writing the book, namely that, although he had never himself been anywhere near the Henares, he had been inspired by what he had heard about Alcalá and its river from a friend who was a native of those parts. It may be noted that the routine use of violent action, more suited to a novel of adventure and intrigue, as well as the circumstantial concern (even if based only on hearsay) with actual geographical locations, both furnish a further instance of how the pastoral novel was shedding the ideal pastoral vision of its inception to merge increasingly with materials from other types of fiction and with concrete particulars from the everyday world, dressed up in pastoral fashion.

7 *Bernardo de la Vega: El Pastor de Iberia* (The Shepherd of Iberia) Seville, 1591.

The author was, according to the title page, "a gentleman from Andalusia." He must, at least for some years, have led a rather agitated existence if it is true, as claimed, that the book narrates actual events. Filardo (the author's "mask"), suspected of having killed a man in a fight, is seized by the authorities. Released thanks to the intervention of friends in high places in Seville, he sails from Sanlúcar de Barrameda for the Canary Islands, where he is again seized, and again released through some effective intervention. His beloved Marfisa avenges (mistakenly, as it turns out) the murder of Tirseo by killing a certain Linardo. There are plenty of alarums and excursions, involving jails, narrow escapes, and confrontations. At the end, however, Filardo and Marfisa marry, and all is well.

There is nothing pastoral about this novel, nor about its setting. The involvement with the contemporary social and historical context is total (there is even a mention of a landing of French troops). The pastoral element does not extend beyond the names of the main characters and a few trees and meadows here and there. This is a more extreme example of what has already been observed in *The Nymphs and Shepherds of the Henares*: a thin pastoral veneer is used as a fashionable device, but none of the substance and character of true pastoral remain. In fact, *The Shepherd of Iberia* hardly qualifies for inclusion in a survey of the genre to which it has traditionally been ascribed, more—one suspects—on account of its title than of its content.

8 *Jerónimo de Covarrubias Herrera: Los Cinco Libros Intitulados la Enamorada Elisea* (The Five Books Entitled Enamored Elisea) Valladolid, 1594.

The title page informs us that the author was a "citizen of the town of Medina de Rioseco residing at Valladolid." He is not otherwise known. Of the five Books, only the first three are devoted to the novel proper. Book IV comprises five separate eclogues and a narrative poem on the *The Loves of Florisauro and Alcida*. Book V (rather like the last Book of Lofrasso's *Fortuna de Amor*) is an anthology of poems. The novel is a standard product of the genre. For inspiration it goes back to Montemayor, rather than to subsequent pastoral authors. It also reveals a good humanistic knowledge of classical literature, as well as an inclination to display literary and linguistic skills (such as the composition of a bilingual sonnet in Spanish and Italian). Its one unusual feature is the location of the action, somewhat startlingly, on the banks of the Nile. This results in certain anachronisms, such as an Egyptian shepherdess referring unembarrassedly to "our Spanish nation." While the Egyptian setting was no doubt inspired by Heliodorus' *Ethiopian Story*, much of whose action happens on the Nile, it is interesting to note that Covarrubias uses none of the adventurous devices of Greek romances. The course of the story runs smoothly and gently. It is an unexciting, but pleasing piece of work, especially in its easy and mellifluous verse. Unlike its two immediate predecessors, it is placed well within the bucolic tradition, and shows at the same time an awareness of the wider scope of that tradition beyond the strictly Spanish context. The choice of the Nile for its setting, rather than a specifically Spanish locality as in the other novels, may be seen as a deliberate attempt to return to the atemporal, ideal world proper to pastoral: a mythical Egypt which is the equivalent of the mythical Arcadia.

9 *Gaspar Mercader: El Prado de Valencia:* (The Pleasance of Valencia) Valencia, 1600.

Gaspar Mercader, Count of Buñuel (1567–1631), was a Valencian nobleman who wrote a good deal of verse, and at one time joined one of the literary academies that, following the Italian example, were burgeoning in Spain as well as in France. This one, the *Academia de los Nocturnos*, active in Valencia from 1591 to 1594, included all the leading Valencian poets, and was one of the most renowned. It also provided the motive for Mercader's writing of the novel a few years later, since *The Pleasance of Valencia* is, to a large extent, an anthology of the poetry produced by the members of the academy. Mercader himself (as Fideno) and his friends appear, thinly disguised under pastoral names, as characters in the novel. The plot is extremely tenuous even by pastoral standards. Of the three books which compose the novel, the first two are almost exclusively anthological. In the third, the action, centering round Olimpio's wish to marry Dinarda and her parents' opposition, develops a little, but is quickly brought to a happy ending. The main setting is the Prado, or pleasance, of the city of Valencia, on the left bank of the river Turia, opposite the city. This is where meetings and partings take place, poems are recited, and artistic or sentimental matters discussed.

For purposes of pastoral color, Mercader exploits the ambiguity between the primary meaning of the word *prado* (a field or meadow), and its secondary meaning as an (urban) pleasure-ground or promenade.[6] There are constant comings and goings between "los pastores del Prado" (the shepherds of the field/pleasance) and "los caballeros de la ciudad" (the gentlemen of the city). They are, of course, the same persons, now in their everyday form, now in their pastoral "mask." Sometimes the "mask" and the person meet face to face, as when "Fideno" and "Don Gaspar Mercader" make arrangements for a poetic festival to be held in the latter's town residence. This does not, however, raise deeper problems of identity, but simply underlines the conventional, *ad hoc* nature of the pastoral characters: they are roles, briefly acted out (rather like the "eclogues" often performed in pastoral novels) on the banks of the river. *The Pleasance of Valencia* is chiefly important as a poetic document of the Valencian school of poetry at the end of the sixteenth century. As a novel, though written in pleasant, easily flowing prose, it is of very little interest and just barely qualifies for inclusion in the pastoral category.

10 *Juan Arze Solórzeno: Tragedias de Amor* (Tragedies of Love) Madrid, 1607.

Juan Arze Solórzeno (1579–?), known otherwise as the author of two devotional works, claimed to have written other pastoral compositions in addition to those included in *Tragedies of Love*, but they do not seem to have ever reached publication. The full title of the novel constitutes a program in itself: *Tragedies of Love, for Pleasant and Peaceable Entertainment with Stories, Fables, Involved Entan-glements, Songs, Dances, and Ingenious Moralities of Enamored Acrisio and his Shepherdess Lucidora.* Here is, in a nutshell, every-thing the reader would expect in a pastoral novel. What is unusual is that the book should be about *tragedies* of love. The characteristic note of pastoral, for all the despairing professions of unrequited lovers, is melancholy, elegiac, but not normally tragic. And these tragedies of love are not without their violent episodes, reminiscent of the technique used by Cervantes to generate suspense and variety. They are, however, not to be taken too tragically, since they are presented for the purpose of "pleasant and peaceable entertain-ment," hardly in the character of true tragedy. In any case, and this is another unique feature in a pastoral novel, the tragedies are to be regarded allegorically, as "ingenious moralities." And Arze Solórzeno duly furnishes a series of interpretations in which the previously narrated events are expounded in terms of moral allegory.

A didactic purpose was not necessarily incompatible with the pastoral novel. On the contrary, we have seen it at work in Gil Polo, in Lope de Vega, and more markedly in López de Enciso. But to present the whole novel as an allegory places it in a rather different category. From this to the entire religious allegorization of the genre in the versions of pastoral *a lo divino* (see Part II of this chapter) there was only one step. Never too far below the surface, the disillusioned, moralizing element in Spanish sensibility and thought had been growing in strength in the post-Tridentine atmosphere of the late sixteenth century, and was to inform much of the literature of the seventeenth. Arze Solórzeno's novel reflects this climate in the field of pastoral. The technique of first telling a story and then explaining its "morality" (essentially, of course, an ecclesiastical preaching de-vice) had been thoroughly tried out precisely in the few years preced-ing the publication of *Tragedies of Love* in two examples of a compet-ing genre: the picaresque novel. Both Mateo Alemán's *Guzmán de Alfarache* (1st Part, 1599; 2nd Part, 1604) and López de Ubeda's *La pícara Justina* (1605) give, at the end of each chapter, a moral inter-pretation of the action just narrated, and Arze Solórzeno may well have borrowed the idea from them.

11 *Bernardo de Balbuena: Siglo de Oro, en las Selvas de Erifile* (The Golden Age, in the Forests of Erifile) Madrid, 1608.

Bernardo de Balbuena (1568–1627), Bishop of Puerto Rico, born in Spain and brought up in Mexico, wrote two other works in addition to his pastoral novel: *Mexican Greatness* (Mexico, 1604), a poem in praise of Mexico City, and *El Bernardo* (Mexico, 1624), an epic poem imitating Ariosto. His *Golden Age* is, of all the Spanish pastoral novels, the one closest to the Italian humanistic model. The subtitle defines what Balbuena set out to do: *In Which is Described a Pleasant and Strict Imitation of the Pastoral Style of Theocritus, Virgil, and Sannazaro*. The presence of Sannazaro is felt everywhere. The formal structure follows very closely that of the original *Arcadia*. As in Sannazaro, there are twelve chapters, which Balbuena calls *Eclogues*, each composed of a prose section followed by a verse eclogue, but Balbuena inserts additional verse in the prose passages. The general character is, as in Sannazaro, descriptive rather than narrative: there is virtually no plot, nor are there any inset stories or unduly exciting events. The specific imitations are many,[7] both of narrative and descriptive elements (e.g., a magic cave, funeral games, underground journey under supernatural guidance) and of prose passages and poems. The classical sources, which Balbuena knew well at first hand, are mainly Virgil's *Eclogues*, as might be expected, but also occasionally his *Georgics* and the *Aeneid*. Theocritus seems to have been mentioned mainly in recognition of his status as the fountainhead of the whole pastoral tradition, rather than on account of any "pleasant and strict imitation" to be found in the novel. However, the *Epistle to the Reader* (not, in this case, by the author himself, but forming part of the laudatory preliminaries contributed by friends of the author) gives an interesting justification: Balbuena has followed Theocritus "inasmuch as the eclogues are free of any allegorical meaning, and Virgil (apart from specific materials) "in preserving the decorum of the persons introduced into his eclogues." As to the language, Balbuena's "poetic prose," as the Epistle calls it, is justified in terms of the imitation of Sannazaro's elaborate and ornamental prose style.

The imitation of Sannazaro, however, goes still further, and extends to the technique of composition itself. Like Sannazaro, though not so comprehensively, Balbuena assembles materials culled from different sources to form a mosaic of imitation, quotation, allusion, and reminiscence. He quarries materials not only from Sannazaro and Virgil, but also from Petrarch and Ariosto, Garcilaso, Boscán, Lomas Cantoral,[8] and Gálvez de Montalvo's *The Shepherd of Filida*. Like many other authors of pastoral novels, Balbuena presented *Golden Age* as an early exercise in literary composition, and it has been suggested that at least a first draft may date back to the early 1580s.[9] Be that as it may, what came out in 1608 was a highly polished literary text which in no way suggests the handiwork of a beginner. The poetry is especially good and, although *Golden Age* did not become a best seller, its author did enjoy a full measure of recognition from his peers, earning warm praise from both Cervantes and Lope de Vega.

Balbuena's outstanding quality as a writer lies in his gift for description. His nature descriptions are striking for their richness and variety. They reflect Sannazaro's descriptive techniques[10] and perhaps also (one may speculate) the effect, on a mind inclined to richly ornamented description, of the luxuriant tropical vegetation of Mexico which he had known from early youth. In this connection, it is interesting to note where he stands in relation to the old dichotomy of nature versus art. For Balbuena, nature is no longer, as for Montemayor, the perfect, self-sufficient manifestation of an ideal world; nor, as in Cervantes, "God's steward," with which man's art may compete or blend, but which it cannot of itself surpass. Here, as was already happening in Lope de Vega, the center has shifted further, and there is a conviction that "artistic reality is superior to physical reality."[11] Hence the tendency, characteristic of the emerging sensibility of the seventeenth century (of which Góngora was to become the most superb example) to describe nature in terms of art, so that it becomes a magnificent artifact deriving its ultimate significance from the writer's imagination.

12 *Cristóbal Suárez de Figueroa: La Constante Amarilis* (Constant Amaryllis) Valencia, 1609.

Cristóbal Suárez de Figueroa (Valladolid, c.1572–Italy? after 1633) was a lawyer by profession, and spent much of his adult life serving as a legal officer with the Spanish authorities in various parts of Italy. As a writer, he produced half a dozen works, most of them from 1604 onward, when he returned to Spain for a time to try, without much success, to make a place for himself in the world of letters. He translated into Spanish Battista Guarini's influential pastoral drama *Il Pastor Fido*.

Constant Amaryllis is again one of those pastoral novels that arise directly from actual events. Its four *Discourses* tell the story of Menandro (Don Juan Andrés Hurtado de Mendoza) and his first cousin Amarilis (Doña Maria de Cárdenas), his family's opposition to their marriage because of the blood relationship, the lovers' success in obtaining a papal dispensation, and their happy marriage. This is filled out with two brief inset stories and many digressions. These comprise most of the standard topics,[12] and some which are more particularly this author's own, such as a rhetorical set-piece in praise of work, a speech on the impermanence of youth and beauty, and an apocalyptic vision of the end of the world. The selection of a wide variety of topics reflects the conception of poetry as a sort of universal science which we have already encountered in Lope de Vega. Like Lope, Suárez de Figueroa thinks of himself as a *poeta eruditus*, and believes that the poet must be conversant with the principles of the liberal arts and all other sciences. Hand in hand with this goes, as in Balbuena, the tendency to grant art, i.e., human artifice, superiority over nature. Suárez de Figueroa's nature descriptions are sensitively wrought, but they are of sites where, as he himself puts it, "art seemed to conquer nature"—parks and gardens, not woods and fields. It is, in Avalle-Arce's apt phrase, a "naturaleza ajardinada,"[13] a nature landscaped by man.

Suárez de Figueroa explained elsewhere[14] that the novel (in which he appears as Damón) was a lukewarm effort, reluctantly written on specific commission. In spite of this disclaimer, it shows all the marks of careful composition, and is clearly the work of a man with a well-stocked mind and considerable literary gifts. The writing, both in prose and in verse, is of remarkable quality throughout the book, well deserving Cervantes' praise (which Suárez de Figueroa, whose ill-nature was proverbial, requited with sneers).

Constant Amaryllis is unusual in the pastoral tradition in its sustained awareness of the transience of human things, and consequent note of general disillusionment. This, while no doubt in part reflecting the author's sour personal disposition, is also a manifestation of the characteristic temper of the Spanish seventeenth century, the century of *desengaño* (disillusionment). With Suárez de Figueroa, the pastoral novel had moved far from the essentially life-affirming nature of its original vision. López de Enciso, it is true, had written *Disillusionment of Jealousy* a good twenty years before; disillusion with sexual love had been the theme of Lope de Vega's *Arcadia*, but only as a positive encouragement to the pursuit of more solid achievements. But Suárez de Figueroa was striking an entirely new note in pastoral when he wrote: "In the wretchedness of my condition, I very often consider what a heavy burden life is, not because I lose courage amid its shipwrecks, but because I see clearly before me the weakness of my being, for it is a foolish thing to forget our own mortality."[15]

13 *Jacinto de Espinel Adorno: El Premio de la Constancia y Pastores de Sierra Bermeja* (The Reward of Constancy and the Shepherds of Sierra Bermeja) Madrid, 1620.

This author was the nephew of Vicente Espinel (1550–1624), the well-known novelist, poet, and musician who gave his name to a type of stanza (the *espinela*) and wrote one of the more attractive of picaresque novels, the largely autobiographical *Marcos de Obregón*. *The Reward of Constancy*, Espinel Adorno's only known work, is set in his native landscapes. Both his birthplace, Manilva, and the town of Ronda, where he grew up, lie on the slopes of the Sierra Bermeja or Red Mountains in Andalusia. The novel, mainly about the loves and adventures of the partly autobiographical Arsindo, runs through most of the usual gamut, including inset tales (two of them mythological, from Ovid's *Metamorphoses*), descriptions of natural scenery, praises of country life, song contests, games, an allegorical dream, a disputation on the qualities of women, a perfunctory philosophical nod in the general direction of Neoplatonism, and, rather more prosaically, disquisitions on the healthy use of physical punishment in bringing up children, and on moderation in drinking. Excitement is provided by the protagonist's experiences, first in the telling of his past history, full of love intrigues, violent action, and reversals of circumstances and later, as the book moves towards its climax, in his being supernaturally carried off in a cloud during a great storm, landing in Africa, and freeing king Celimo from a magic spell (we are reminded of Anfriso's magic flight in Lope de Vega's *Arcadia*, but in a more carefree mood of pure storytelling). An inclination to experiment with different types of poetry is very much in evidence but the verse seldom rises above mediocrity. The prose, on the other hand, except for a certain tendency to overelaboration, is clear and self-assured, and the book makes pleasant, entertaining reading. It is, however, another of those novels whose pastoralism is merely nominal. Through its established formal characteristics, the pastoral convention supplies a convenient framework for the materials the author wishes to include, but the specific pastoral vision is nowhere in evidence.

14 *Miguel Botello: Prosas y Versos del Pastor de Clenarda* (Proses and Verses of the Shepherd of Clenarda). Madrid, 1622.

Like Montemayor, Miguel Botelho de Carvalho (Viseu 1595–after 1654) was a Portuguese who chose to write in Castilian and modified his name's spelling accordingly. He had a distinguished career, both military and civilian, in the Portuguese service, and published several volumes of verse, sacred and profane (including a long pastoral poem) in addition to *The Shepherd of Clenarda*.

The novel's main plot concerns Lisardo's and Clenarda's successful love affair, only slightly troubled by purely external events: their marriage has to be temporarily postponed when he is sent to Madrid on business. On his return, the merry wedding takes place and the book ends. One cannot but contrast this happy state of affairs with that which confronted Sireno, similarly sent away "about certain affairs," on his return to the valley of the Ezla in Montemayor. Botello fills out this uneventful framework with two inset tales of love and intrigue, set in Madrid and in Toledo, and with various digressions and displays of erudition and literary skill, including the ubiquitous paraphrase of Horace's *Beatus ille* (in prose instead of verse), a discourse on jealousy, a few Neoplatonic references, a series of delicate compliments to contemporary authors, and so on. No consciously formulated ideology is apparent, but the underlying assumptions are similar to those we have found in Balbuena and Suárez de Figueroa. Nature is no longer divine, a demiurge, or "God's steward"; Heaven dispenses its benefits without intermediary. Nature descriptions are elaborated in careful literary terms, harking back to the exquisite bucolism of Sannazaro. Well over a century after its publication, the original *Arcadia* continued to loom large in the world of the pastoral writer. The literary qualities of *The Shepherd of Clenarda*, both in prose and in verse, are modest.

15 *Manuel Fernández Raya: Esperanza Engañada* (Hope Deceived) Coimbra, 1624.

This was not included in Rennert's or Avalle-Arce's surveys, but W. F. King drew attention to it as a late pastoral novel.[16] Having been unable to see it, we can only record its existence and hope that a study of it can soon be made.

16 *Juan Enríquez de Zúñiga: Amor con Vista* (Love with Eyes) Madrid, 1625.

This (which was also brought to attention by W. F. King) is one of several works and the only pastoral effort from the pen of Juan Enríquez de Zúñiga, born in Guadalajara, mayor of Cuenca and doctor of canon and civil law. As the title indicates, this is not about *blind* love, but about the rational, sensible kind that keeps its eyes wide open, and about lovers who "without loving any the less than those of the past, never allowed inclination to tyrannize understanding." The plot is that of a typical novel of love and intrigue, with complications due to mistaken identities and misinterpreted situations, and a happy ending in which everyone gets a suitable partner through reasonable, agreed arrangements. The pastoral characters all turn out, explicitly, to be ladies and gentlemen in disguise and the whole work is treated openly as a piece of light entertainment. Except for one mythological tale, all the inset stories are ramifications of the central plot. The second of the three parts is taken up by a long digression: a satirical dream containing a "description of the world." Otherwise, the presentation is concise and well-knit, the various plot elements being developed and combined with skill. The prose is functional, clear, and simple, and the poetry competent, resulting in a work which makes entertaining reading. It is marked by a pleasing absence of sentimentality and by a supremely reasonable tone which often sounds like a prefiguration of eighteenth-century rationalism.

17 *Jerónimo de Tejeda: Third Part* to Montemayor's *Diana*. Paris, 1627.

We now come to a work mainly notable as a monumental example of plagiarism by a Castilian interpreter living in Paris. As a reason for writing his *Diana*, Tejeda explained in the introduction that the original work (by which he means both Montemayor's *Diana*, as the "First Part," and Alonso Pérez's as the "Second") had been given fanciful sequels by French publishers which were far in intent and plot from the originals. Hence he, Tejeda, had now decided to bring the tales to a proper conclusion. To achieve this end without unduly straining his own powers of invention, he resorted to wholesale plagiarism, mainly of Gil Polo (whose very existence he carefully refrained from mentioning), and also of Cervantes, Lope de Vega, and even Lofrasso.

Roughly the first half of Tejeda's *Diana* is almost entirely composed of barely disguised materials taken straight—sometimes almost word for word—from Gil Polo's *Diana enamorada*. The remainder of the book is somewhat freer, but still substantially indebted to other authors. Several of the many inset stories are more or less closely inspired by plots or materials in Cervantes (both from *Galatea* and *Don Quixote*), Montemayor, and several of Lope de

Vega's historical plays. As for the poetry, it is mostly from Gil Polo, but there are also many poems from plays by Lope de Vega, several from Cervantes' *Galatea*, and one from Lofrasso's *Fortune of Love*.[17] Tejeda's own contribution consists mainly in the task of compilation, paraphrase, and arrangement.

This indifferently written re-hash adds nothing to literature, and little to the history of the pastoral genre. What little there is of ideas or debates is as derivative as the plots. As a revealing pointer to the prevailing mental climate as one moves further into the seventeenth century, one may note that in Tejeda the reversal in roles in the old confrontation between nature and art is now complete: the beauty of some trees, for instance, is stressed by saying that "they seemed rather to have been planted there by the industry and work of man, than produced by nature," and the highest praise that can be bestowed on a meadow is to say that it looks like "a curious and artfully woven carpet."[18]

18 *Gabriel de Corral: La Cintia de Aranjuez* (Cynthia of Aranjuez) Madrid, 1629.

Gabriel de Corral (Valladolid, 1588–Toro, 1646), a distinguished ecclesiastic, was a well-known literary figure, renowned especially as an excellent Latinist and scholar. From him one might well have expected a strenuous show of erudition. The *Prologue*, with its learned prose style and abundant Latin quotations, does little to dispel that expectation. But it also stresses that this is a work of entertainment addressed "to the common people," and quotes two verses from Góngora: "I seek the applause of the people/and may the Tribunes forgive me." And Corral is as good as his word. The novel that follows is written quite straightforwardly, with no pedantry or recondite allusions. It moves, on the whole, swiftly and entertainingly with few digressions. The inset tales concern the two main characters, Fileno and Cintia, and Fileno's sister, Alexandra, and are directly relevant to the progress of the main plot. The plot itself is intricate, relying on disguises and mistaken identities. *Cynthia of Aranjuez* is best described as a novel of intrigue and suspense revolving around the willful female protagonist's initial refusal to marry her family's choice, the happy ending resulting from the discovery that her newly formed attachment to a stranger (Fileno) in fact coincides with her expected duty.

As may be imagined from this, the love interest is kept at a practical, down-to-earth level, with little room for love philosophies. On the other hand, the course of the action is embellished and sometimes severely held up by several set-pieces which are mainly pretexts for groups of poems, including a verse eclogue, two long series of epigrams, two poetry competitions (one of them consisting of glosses on verses by Góngora), a satirically allegorical Hospital for Poets, an epithalamium, and the great courtly festivities at the end on an artificial island in the middle of the river Jarama, with complex machinery to effect all sorts of cunningly devised transformations (exactly of the kind that were becoming intensely popular on the stage, especially in performances of allegorical, religious and miracle plays). These comprise, among others, a mountain that turns into a castle, singing sirens and floating musicians, a seven-headed, fire-breathing sea serpent, and Perseus on a winged Pegasus, culminating in a final transformation into a beautiful garden with a sumptuous banquet all laid out.

   Cynthia of Aranjuez is well written, more so in its smooth, flexible prose than in its verse. Gabriel de Corral especially admired the easy-flowing style of Góngora's poems in popular modes, and it was on this that he strove to model many of his own poems. The result has an easy charm and is mellifluous enough, but hardly memorable. He also occasionally tried his hand, with rather less success, at the intricate "high" style of Góngora's more ambitious verse. The novel is presented primarily as a vehicle for the author's verse ("all the verses contained in this volume were already written before the attempt and, to make them tolerable, I set them in these proses"). On the other hand, the claim to be writing a true story in disguise is, for once, not made. Yet, although the complex and occasionally violent intrigues are no doubt literary inventions, there may well be a core of real events to the story. There would otherwise be little point in the explicit identification of all the main characters given in the novel itself. Cintia is Doña Guiomar de Guzmán, a member of one of the great noble houses of Castile, the most eminent representative of which was the Count-Duke of Olivares, favorite of King Philip IV. Significantly, it is this powerful relative of the heroine, rather than Corral's current patron and employer (to whom the book is nominally dedicated) who is the subject of the panegyric portions of the novel.

   But what, one may ask, is the role of pastoral in all this? The answer is that, by this time, the pastoral element has run the full course from philosophical ideal to conventional entertainment. Here there is no question at all of the characters being any kind of shepherds, idealized or not. They are quite explicitly young ladies and young men-about-town who are keeping Cintia company for a while on her luxurious country estate at Aranjuez, and who have decided to dress up as shepherds "in the fictitious Arcadia which they instituted" on the banks of the river Jarama, so as to while away the time as agreeably as possible in this "pastoral Academy" with poetry, music, and theatrical performances (and also, occasionally, with more exciting pastimes such as bull-baiting by the gentlemen). At the end, the ladies and gentlemen return to Madrid, and "some folk from the neighboring villages, partly drawn by curiosity, and partly by the pleasantness of the spot, came to occupy . . . the deserted shepherd's huts." The dream had become a game; the game is over, and everyday life reasserts its rights.

19 *Gonzalo de Saavedra: Los Pastores del Betis* (The Shepherds of the Betis) Trani, 1633.

According to the information furnished by the author's son, who published the novel posthumously, Gonzalo de Saavedra (Cordoba 1573/75–1623/33) had written *The Shepherds of the Betis* in his youth; most of the shepherds in it were "noble persons" who used to belong to a literary academy established in Granada in the years 1603–1604; and "almost the majority of the discourses and endeavors described therein" were true. On this evidence, this novel would be a compilation of literary academy material not unlike that of Gaspar Mercader, and not much later in date of writing. We do not know to what extent the son modified the original text, since he did point out (in the title, but without further specification elsewhere) that he had "added some fragments of his own." In any case, it is an unexciting and somewhat old-fashioned specimen of the genre. It bears the clear imprint of Sannazaro (mentioned in the son's introduction as the authority on pastoral matters) in its nature descriptions and especially in the latter part of the book, which is inspired by the final prose of the Italian *Arcadia*. Here again are the expected wanderings, meetings and partings of shepherds and shepherdesses, a visit to the temple of Diana, as well as the chains of lovers and the stress on the operation of fate and fortune which were a feature of early pastoral novels. Further evidence of an earlier mental climate is found in the references to "maestra naturaleza," or nature as a teacher, a conception which, as we have seen, had been gradually replaced, from the late sixteenth century, by that of the superiority of man and his artifacts. Gonzalo de

Saavedra's prose style aims to be ornately polished, but errs more often than not on the side of verbosity and confusion. The poetry is formally competent enough, and entirely forgettable. If it in fact represents a cross-section of the work produced at Granada in the early 1600s, the poets of that literary academy would seem to have been on the whole clearly inferior to those of the Valencian academy represented in Gaspar Mercader's pages.

20 *Ana Francisca Abarca de Bolea. Vigilia y Octavario de San Juan Bautista* (Vigil and Octave of Saint John the Baptist) Saragossa, 1679.

The Shepherds of the Betis had long been regarded as the last Spanish pastoral novel. Yet, since M. Alvar and W. F. King drew attention to Abarca de Bolea's *Vigil and Octave*,[19] account must also be taken of this late, and probably truly last, specimen of a vanishing breed. Its author, who belonged to the high nobility of Aragon, was a Cistercian abbess who combined religious with literary interests. This novel was her only excursion into the field of secular or primarily secular writing. Rather like the novels of Fernández Raya and Enríquez de Zúñiga, but for different reasons, it has not in the past been included in discussions of the Spanish pastoral novels, as there has been a tendency to regard it as a religious pastoral of the kind that we shall consider in a moment. Not entirely without justification, in view of the writer's religious status, the religious tone of the title and the devotional character of the frame situation: the celebration of a religious festival. However, the focus is clearly on the bustle of worldly affairs, and the characters themselves, though pious, are firmly concerned with matters of this world, without any suggestion of transcendental or allegorical meanings. It seems therefore more reasonable to include *Vigil and Octave* among the secular pastoral novels.

The pastoral plot is tenuous in the extreme, and diluted by constant digressions. The pretext, as the title suggests, is simple enough: a group of wealthy shepherds decide to celebrate the festivity of Saint John the Baptist by observing an octave: for eight days, including the festival itself and its day week, they hear Mass every morning in a country chapel, and after the appropriate devotions spend the rest of the day in entirely secular festivities and pastimes. Each member of the group in turn organizes one day's amusements. These include sumptuous picnics, a bullfight, storytelling (there are two inset tales and several brief anecdotes), debates, songs, dances and poetry competitions, and, as *pièce de résistance*, an account of the virtues and qualities of the figure seven, with no less than seven hundred examples from biblical, historical, and other sources. The love interest runs an uneventful course. On the seventh day, three of the shepherds ask their respective lady loves in marriage, and are accepted. The pastoral mask is entirely transparent and most of the shepherds no doubt represent real persons from the literary circles with which the authoress was connected and whose poems are copiously anthologized in the novel. It is interesting to note that, as in Mercader, the authoress appears not only in her pastoral mask, but also in her own character as a religious (to whom the other characters often refer in eulogistic terms—hardly a display of becoming modesty). The writing is merely competent.

II   Versions *"a lo divino"*

Writing *a lo divino* (literally, "in divine terms") has been defined as "religious parody, or the rewriting of profane literature in religious terms." [20] The production of divinized versions of popular songs by altering existing profane lyrics to suit the new purpose, or replacing them entirely with religious lyrics written to the original popular melody, had long been an accepted practice in certain countries. [21] In Spain, the flowering of literature in the sixteenth century was accompanied by a growth of the practice, reflecting the literary puritanism which is one of the factors running through the century (accentuated in its latter part by the doctrinal and intellectual effects of the Council of Trent). Not only folk songs, but poetry of all kinds was subjected to the treatment. Some poets, such as Juan del Encina, rewrote their own poems. Others adapted those of other authors. A major effort of this kind was that of a certain Sebastian de Córdoba, who recast the complete works of Boscán and Garcilaso in a religious mold. [22]

Divinization, while flourishing mainly in the field of song and poetry, was only seldom applied to whole prose works, possibly because of the more sustained effort required in dealing with extended forms. In view of the integral connection of pastoral imagery with the Christian religious tradition since its earliest origins, however, one might expect pastoral novels to be readier candidates for divinization than any other type of prose. Even here, however, there are in all only three works of this kind.

1 *Bartolomé Ponce: Clara Diana a lo Divino* (Clear Diana in Divine Style) Saragossa, 1599.

"I promise you, my good sir Montemayor—said I—that in my rough and ready vein I shall compose another *Diana* to run after yours and cudgel her with clumsy blows." [23] This was in 1559. Brother Bartolomé Ponce, the Cistercian monk from Aragon, in expressing his admiration to Montemayor, the now-fashionable author, had also "taken courage to point out how he [Montemayor] was wasting his keen understanding, and the other faculties of the soul, spending his time thinking out conceits, measuring rhymes, fabricating stories and composing books on worldly love and in profane style." It was upon Montemayor's laughing repartee that he left penitence to the friars, that Brother Bartolomé came back with the facetious sally just quoted. The anecdote aptly summarizes the motivation behind the efforts to divinize works of secular literature.

For all his talk of cudgeling, Bartolomé Ponce's own effort was mild enough. He did not, in fact, attempt to recast Montemayor's novel, but simply wrote an entirely independent religious allegory in the form of a pastoral novel, which has only the title, and the division into seven Books, in common with the original *Diana*. He no doubt hoped to ride the wave of Montemayor's popularity, an aim which was rather defeated by the greatly delayed publication of *Clear Diana*. The reasons for the delay are unknown, though one may surmise difficulties in obtaining ecclesiastical approval.

Ponce's religious pastoral portrays the struggle between the world, the flesh, and the devil, on the one hand, and the faculties of the soul on the other. The devil is a rich sheepowner, the flesh a shepherdess appropriately named Caro, and the world a young shepherd, her lover. Caro has three sisters (Esquálida, Rutuba, and Felia) who, as explained in the introduction, represent "concupiscencia carnis, concupiscencia oculorum et superbia vite." ("desire of the flesh, desire of the eyes and pride of life") The devil's seven daughters (the seven deadly sins), posing as their friends, encourage Caro and her sisters to sin, but their efforts are opposed by those of seven "divine shepherdesses" who are, of course, the seven cardinal virtues. The protagonist is a shepherd called Barpolio standing for "rational man," whose flocks are his thoughts and passions, and whose proper concern should be to watch over and control them, and to remain faithful to "his shepherdess, the Soul."

That this kind of allegory, uninviting though it may at first appear to a modern mind unused to thinking in such terms, could produce deeply moving works of great intellectual power was to be magnificently demonstrated by Calderón in his religious-allegorical *autos sacramentales*. Brother Bartolomé Ponce's gifts as a writer, however, were insignificant. He spoke more truly than he intended, no doubt, when modestly referring to the "clumsiness" of the *Diana* he was planning. His writing is heavy and pedestrian and weighed down with erudite quotations, allusions, and references to a degree that would seriously hinder even a much more competent style.

2 *Lope de Vega: Los Pastores de Belén, Prosas y Versos Divinos* (The Shepherds of Bethlehem, Divine Proses and Verses) Lérida 1612.

Lope de Vega also related his religious pastoral novel back to Montemayor, by paraphrasing in its first sentence the opening of the original *Diana*. But this, like Ponce's title, is merely by way of formal acknowledgment, and the novel goes its own way thereafter. The five books of *The Shepherds of Bethlehem* are not allegorical, but biblical in subject matter, being a treatment of the Nativity and related events up to the Flight into Egypt. As so often in the Nativity plays whose tradition it carries on, the novel's opening scenes demonstrate the expectancy generated by prophecies concerning the birth of a Savior. There follow then the Nativity, the Adoration of the Shepherds, the Adoration of the Magi, and the Flight into Egypt. Variety is sought by introducing inset stories, which are here especially plentiful, and all taken from the Bible.

The novel closes with the author once again, as he had done in his *Arcadia*, bidding farewell to his rustic pipe. In this epilogue he stresses the palinodic character of the book, and this was more than a formal gesture. It was written as Lope, just turning fifty, was taking stock of a life in which, while achieving great literary successes, he had also experienced much personal bitterness, heartbreak, and disappointment. He had always been, for all his wild behavior, a truly religious person, and was to take holy orders soon after, in 1614. *The Shepherds of Bethlehem* must be seen in the context of his efforts at reorientation and spiritual consolidation during those years. As a work of literature it is remarkably successful. It contains many exquisite lyrics and is infused with a sense of reverence and tenderness, especially toward the figure of the Virgin Mary. It enjoyed consider-

able success, but certain passages, such as the story of Susanna and
the Elders, were expunged by the Inquisition on account of what was
felt to be their excessive eroticism.

3 *Francisco Bramón: Los Sirgueros de la Virgen sin Original Pecado*
   (The Goldfinches of the Virgin without Original Sin) Mexico,
   1620.[24]

This is a work of Marian devotion written by a Mexican scholar and
priest. It is in three Books, describing the preparations for, and the
holding of, festivities in celebration of the mystery of the Immaculate
Conception of the Virgin Mary, culminating in the performance of an
allegorical play enacting the failure of Original Sin to taint the purity
of the Virgin. The author of the play and protagonist of the book is
Anfriso, Bramón's "mask" and prime mover of the festivities, who is
spending a few days' relaxation between university examinations with
a group of "feigned" shepherds not far from Mexico City. Although
some of the entertainments organized are secular enough—fire-
works, bullfights—and a very mild, utterly proper love affair is
sketched in between Menandro and Arminda, the religious, devotional tone is held firmly throughout: shepherds and shepherdesses
meditate on original sin, hold theological debates, explain the sym-
bols of Marian devotion, see visions of the Virgin in their dreams, and
sing songs in honor of her Immaculate Conception. Anfriso declares
to Florinarda that he loves not her but the Virgin Mary. Formally and
stylistically, the work follows the well established patterns of pastoral
novels. The prose is heavy and ornate, the verse moderate. The play
which takes up virtually the whole of Book III is a competent example
of the religious allegorical dramatic genre which was to culminate in
the magnificent *autos sacramentales* of Calderón.

III *Marginal Works*

There are a few works of literary fiction in the Spanish sixteenth
and seventeenth centuries which, while having some connection
with pastoral, do not fall within the purview of this study, either
because they are pastoral, but not novels, or novels where the pastoral element is too marginal to be of significance. However, as several
of them have been included in past surveys of pastoral, they are
briefly listed here to clarify the issue in each case.

1. *Jerónimo de Arbolanche*: *Los nueve libros de las Habidas* (The Nine Books of Abido's Adventures) Saragossa 1566.

This was included by Rennert in his *Spanish Pastoral Romances* on the strength of a statement by a nineteenth-century scholar, P. Gayangos,[25] to the effect that it was "one among the earliest imitations of the *Diana*," though Rennert did caution that "it is written wholly in verse." [26] Avalle-Arce excluded it from his survey with the comment: "it is not a novel—it is a poem with little that is bucolic about it." [27] In fact, it is a verse romance of chivalry which develops the theme of the king's son, abandoned in infancy, who survives and returns to claim his rightful throne. The pastoral element is provided by Abido's growing up among the shepherds who found him as a child, and includes a love affair with a shepherdess.

2. *Captain Flegetonte* (a pseudonym): *La Cryselia de Lidaceli* (Cryselia of Lidaceli) Paris, 1609.

The subtitle, *A Story of Various Events of Love and Arms*, suggests that the pastoral element is purely adventitious. This is mentioned by Avalle-Arce, but with the comment that it "should be studied as a romance of chivalry, rather than as a pastoral novel." [28]

3. *Francisco de las Cuevas*: *Experiencias de amor y fortuna* (Experiences of Love and Fortune) Madrid, 1626.

This, also written under a pseudonym (the author's real name was Francisco Quintana), used also at one time (like *Las Habidas*) to be described as a pastoral novel, which it is not. Notwithstanding a slight pastoral note in the opening—a main character in the guise of a shepherd, and a briefly sketched bucolic setting—it is purely a novel of adventure.[29]

4. *Juan de Barrionuevo y Moya*: *Segunda Parte de la Soledad entretenida* (Second Part of Solitude with Entertainment) Valencia, 1644.[30]

Although W. F. King classifies this with some qualification as a pastoral novel, it has in fact only a thin veneer of pastoral. It tells the exemplary story of "a strong young man, and courageous, not only in controlling others, but in controlling and overcoming himself with temperance, with chastity and with many other virtues." [31] It also provides the pretext for inserting four plays on legendary historical subjects.

5. *Fernando Jacinto de Zurita y Haro: Méritos disponen premios, discurso lírico* (Merits Command Prizes: Lyrical Discourse) Madrid, 1654.

This is a curious tour de force—a novel written entirely without using the letter *a*, hardly a recommendation of literary worth. W.F. King [32] writes: "It is a *novela cortesana* (a novel of amorous intrigue) in everything except the characters' clothes."

CHAPTER 7

Conclusion

THE success of the pastoral novels did not fail to generate hostil-
ity. The main attacks came from ecclesiastical quarters and were
motivated by concern at the morally debilitating effect of such attrac-
tively presented love literature. Suspicion was sharpened in the age
of the Counter-Reformation by the conspicuous absence of any
Christian elements in these works, even in authors with a serious
moral commitment, such as Gil Polo. As early as 1565, father confes-
sors were thundering about "fictions which under pastoral garb and
style conceal the kind of ugliness that goes on at court." The classic
condemnation came in the prologue to *La conversión de la Magda-
lena* (*The Conversion of Mary Magdalene,* 1585) by the Augustinian
Pedro Malón de Chaide, specifically written as a morally sound
alternative to those "wordly lascivious books . . . For what else are
books about love, and Dianas, Boscans and Garcilasos . . . [as well as
the romances of chivalry] . . ., placed in young hands, but like unto a
knife in the hands of a wild, irresponsible man?" [1] We have seen (ch.
6,II) that other moralists, like Fr. Bartolomé Ponce, tried to divert,
rather than oppose, the tide by producing "divinized" pastoral literature. But the attempt did not prosper much, and the main attitude
continued to be one of denunciation, tempered by the knowledge
that a frontal attack on these well-established favorites was tactically
inadvisable, and no doubt also by the feeling that they were rather
more harmless than one might be inclined to allow in the heat of
pulpit oratory. In fact, for all the ecclesiastical invective and the
suggestions that a bonfire of such books "would be perfume and
incense in the nostrils of saints and lovers of God," the Inquisition did
not find it necessary (with one or two exceptions) [2] to take any
concrete steps against pastoral novels, which continued to be busily
written and read.

In examining the products of this literary activity over a period of
roughly one hundred years, we have observed how different authors

143

made their own characteristic choices to produce works that vary considerably in their commitment to the pastoral ideal and in the degree of literary coherence achieved. It is a far cry from Montemayor's ideal world, skillfully interwoven with adventure and romance, to that of Bernardo de la Vega's low intrigues and tussles with the law in *The Shepherd of Iberia*, or from the plot complexities of *Galatea* to the peaceable descriptive flow of Balbuena's *Golden Age*. As a general trend, it is clear that the pastoral element became increasingly adventitious. The myth, gradually drained of its power, became a game, and the contents of the novels grew more and more openly concerned with the everyday affairs of the world in which and for which they were being written.

The common ground, of course, remained: the basic pastoral love stories (perfunctory though they might become in some cases), frequently claiming to be inspired by fact, and accompanied by discussions on love philosophy, and often also on literary theory. Some of the novels stay entirely, or almost, within this sphere (e.g., *The Shepherd of Filida*, *Enamored Elisea*—for all its Egyptian setting— or Mercader's and Saavedra's poetic anthologies). Beyond this, the kinds of materials used to add variety and interest may roughly be grouped under two headings: narrative, and erudite/ornamental. The former consist essentially of inset stories (inaugurated by Montemayor, pursued by Pérez and Gil Polo, and strongly developed by Cervantes), using incidents and adventures inspired largely by the Greek romances, and plots from a variety of literary sources, such as Italian *novelle*. The erudite/ornamental approach is seen at its most exuberant in Lope de Vega's *Arcadia*, with its masses of pseudoscientific information, mythological tales and allusions, and ornamental episodes and descriptions of various kinds. Balbuena's *Golden Age* and Suárez de Figueroa's *Constant Amaryllis* are preeminently of this type. Some of the authors, finally, such as Alonso Pérez, Lofrasso or López de Enciso, drew freely on both types of resources.

The results of all this literary activity were sometimes felicitous, and sometimes less so; the ability of some authors to organize would at times collapse under the weight of heterogeneous material. But in meeting the challenge, important techniques were being developed and refined. In the crucial matter of narrative technique, for instance, a recent stimulating analysis [3] has drawn attention to the subtle and effective ways in which overall control by a third-person narrator in the primary narrative was combined with first-person interventions (as inset tales), and how secondary actions of relatively long duration, compact and rapidly told (in the first or in the third person), lying in the past, were integrated in the timeless present of the primary pastoral situation. Together with the humanistic prose comedy which was, in effect, a novel in dialogue form (the first great example of which had been *La Celestina* [1499–1502], and with the picaresque novel (starting with the *Lazarillo de Tormes* of 1554), the narrative techniques of the pastoral novel as well as its psychological orientation and ideological content were helping to shape the future course of the European novel. It is no accident that *Don Quixote* (Part I, 1605, Part II, 1615) came out when it did, and that it contained significant pastoral, as well as picaresque, components.

Pastoral novels also made an important contribution to the fashioning of a supple, versatile prose style which would easily adapt to the great variety of subjects to be covered: rich and sonorous for ornamental passages, sharp and elegant in debates, musically reflective for lyrical moods, swift and workmanlike in straight narrative. These qualities, as has been seen, were successfully developed in various ways by Montemayor, Gil Polo, Cervantes, and others. By the time we reach a writer such as Corral, we find him writing in a manner that is strikingly modern in its directness. Yet these were not the only possibilities explored; the highly formalized, rhetorical, and intellectually complex prose of seventeenth-century *culteranismo* was also fed from pastoral sources such as Lope's *Arcadia*. Altogether, it is perfectly accurate to describe sixteenth-century Spain as "an experimental workshop for fiction serving all western Europe," [4] and pastoral novels were among the most successful of its literary products both at home and abroad. Montemayor's *Diana*, the first in time, proved also by far the most popular. By the end of the seventeenth century it had gone through forty editions in Spanish and thirty-one in translations (French, English, German, and Dutch).[5] Its two immediate continuations, carried along in its wake, were soon being issued (especially in translations) together with it, with Pérez's as the "Second" and Gil Polo's as the "Third" Part, often not even identified as by separate authors on the title page, but sailing jointly under Montemayor's name.[6] It is no exaggeration to say that "the Spanish *Diana*," as it became known (with or without the other "Parts"), swept Europe in the original, as much as in translations, since Spanish was for a time the major language of culture and politics. A development to which *Diana*'s own contribution is far from negligible: it set a pattern of sensibility and of literary expression, became a model of style to all who read Spanish, and even a means of learning the language for those who did not, as attested by the series of bilingual editions, with facing Spanish and French texts, published in Paris between 1603 and 1613. As early as 1599, a Spanish-English dictionary drew upon "Wordes, Phrases, Sentences and Proverbes" from *Diana* as grammatical examples.[7]

In France and in England, and later in Germany, the Spanish pastoral novels, and *Diana* in particular (the epitome of the whole genre) contributed much by way of literary attitudes, techniques, and materials to the literatures of those countries. To trace these is a task beyond the present scope and one which, in spite of a fair amount of valuable research into individual aspects, has not yet been comprehensively attempted; mention of a few salient points will have to suffice.[8] In France, Honoré d 'Urfé's *Astrée* (I, 1607; II, 1610; III, 1619; IV and V, 1627), vastly influential throughout Europe, and one of the recognized sources of the modern novel, was itself strongly influenced (in setting, characters, and numerous situations and episodes) by *Diana*. In England, Shakespeare, and Sir Philip Sidney must be mentioned. The latter's *Arcadia* (1590, revised 1593 and 1599), was, as is well known, modeled on *Diana*, and itself again a widely influential book in England and elsewhere (especially in Germany). As for Shakespeare, his familiarity with *Diana* is apparent at many points. It has often been pointed out that the main (Julia-Proteus) plot of *Two Gentlemen of Verona* is taken from Montemayor (and not from the original Bandello story). But there are other borrowings or reminiscences, such as the main plot of *A Midsummernight's Dream*, from Book I of *Diana*, and the use in *Twelfth Night* of elements from Felismena's story not included in *Two Gentlemen of Verona*.[9]

In Germany, Hans Ludwig von Kuffstein's translation of Montemayor and Pérez in 1619, and Georg Philipp Harsdörffer's recasting of this, with the addition of Gil Polo, in 1646 (together with the 1619 translation of Urfé's *Astrée*, and the German versions of Sidney's *Arcadia* in 1630 and 1638), were important vehicles for the dissemination of the newer literary ideals, while Kaspar von Barth's Latin translation of Gil Polo (1625) was a major source of Petrarchan influence on Martin Opitz (1597–1639), the initiator of literary reform in seventeenth-century Germany. It is also worth noting that Harsdörffer was one of the founders of the poetic "order" of the Shepherds of Pegnitz in Nuremberg, a literary academy not unlike those anthologized in *The Pleasance of Valencia* and *The Shepherds of the Betis*.

With regard to the influence of the Spanish pastoral novel on the development of the novel as a genre, the claim has been made that "if from *Diana* is derived *L'Astrée*, and from *L'Astrée* through Prévost, Marivaux, Le Sage one comes to the English novel of Richardson and Fielding, we have then reached exactly the modern novel." [10] As it stands, this is a large over-simplification. Nevertheless, it does contain a substantial element of truth which should not be disregarded in assessing the historical significance of these novels.

What about their intrinsic quality? As we have seen, there is—as in all things—good, bad, and indifferent among them. But out of the twenty-four we have examined [11] Montemayor's and Gil Polo's *Dianas* must rank very high by any valid standards of literary value and human relevance. Cervantes' *Galatea* and Lope de Vega's *Arcadia*, though not unflawed, are unquestionably major achievements which deserve, and richly repay, close attention. Among the rest we have at least a dozen works which, while less fundamental, have much to offer by way of literary quality and sheer entertainment value: *The Shepherd of Filida, Golden Age, Cynthia of Aranjuez, Enamored Elisea, Tragedies of Love, Love with Eyes.* A more than creditable achievement for any body of literature, especially considering that, of the remainder, only a few (e.g., Tejeda's *Diana, The Nymphs and Shepherds of the Henares, The Shepherd of Iberia, The Shepherds of the Betis*) entirely deserve the traditional strictures of artificiality and poor craftsmanship.

This can be more clearly seen now that a number of developments in the twentieth century have helped to clear our minds. The growth of historical perspective in literary criticism, the realization that naive views of realism, and of "sincerity" are entirely inadequate (for one age's "reality" is another's "artifice"), the better-informed access to widely different cultural contexts, the radically experimental approaches to form and content in all branches of art characteristic of our times: these are some of the factors that make it possible for us to recognize in the Spanish pastoral novels the cogency deriving from their root in myth, in the world of archetypes and universal human aspirations, and the literary value of their pursuit of formal qualities in prose and in verse.

Appendix on Versification

Main traditional Spanish and Italianate forms found in pastoral novels.

Arte mayor verse: line of nine or more syllables.

Arte menor verse: line of eight syllables or less.

Canción (*petrarquista* or *a la italiana*): poem composed of stanzas combining hendecasyllables and heptasyllables, with a *remate* (envoy). Metrical and rhyme scheme at poet's choice, but identical for all stanzas. In the regular form, the stanzas are tripartite, following the pattern popularized by Petrarch: *fronte* (itself divided into two halves), *eslabón* (a pivotal line or lines), and closing *sirima*. The final *remate* stanza is usually shorter than the rest (e.g., *FDE*, 74–7).

Canción libre: poem consisting of *silvas*, with or without envoy. Many examples in Lope de Vega.

Copla castellana: octosyllabic eight-line stanza, rhyming *abbacddc*. In effect, two *redondillas*, sense-linked.

Copla de arte mayor: stanza of eight *arte mayor* verses (most commonly dodecasyllables with a caesura). Rhyming usually *ABBAACCA* or *ABABBCCB*. The verse of fifteenth-century learned poetry.

Copla de arte menor: stanza of eight octosyllables, rhyming *abbaacca*. In effect, two *redondillas* with one common rhyme.

Copla real: stanza with ten octosyllables, arranged 5 + 5, equivalent to two *quintillas*, usually with different rhyme schemes. A favorite with Cervantes.

Cuarteta: stanza of four *arte menor* verses, usually rhyming *abab*.

Decima: ten-line stanza (octosyllables, sometimes with tetrasyllables), arranged 4 + 6 or 6 + 4. Four or five rhymes, arranged at will (cf. *espinela*).

Espinela: strict form of *décima*: octosyllabic, rhyming *abba* + *accddc*. Its invention is attributed to Vicente Espinel (1550–1624), the uncle of Espinel Adorno.

Glosa: a gloss on an existing verse or verses, which appear first as motto at the head of the poem. Usually octosyllabic, but no specific formal requirements except that the motto must be integrated into the rhyme pattern. Montemayor, for instance, favors a seven-line stanza rhyming *bccbbaa*, where *aa* are the two verses being glossed. (cf. *villancico*)

Lira: a short Italianate *canción* stanza (usually four to six lines) in heptasyllables and hendecasyllables. The basic form is *aBabB*. Named after the opening line of Garcilaso's *canción 'A la flor de Gnido'*: *"Si de mi baxa lira."* (To the Flower of Gnido: "If my humble lyre's sound")

148

Octava real: (the Italian *ottava rima*): stanza of eight hendecasyllables rhyming *ABABABCC*.

Octavilla: any stanza of eight *arte menor* verses.

Quintilla: stanza of five octosyllables. Possible rhyme combinations: *ababa, abbab, abaab, aabab, aabba*.

Redondilla: stanza of four octosyllables, rhyming either *abba* or *abab*. One of the oldest and most common Spanish verse forms.

Romance: continuous octosyllabic sequence with assonance on the even lines, the same assonance being maintained. The ancient form of Spanish narrative folk-poetry.

Sextilla: stanza of six *arte menor* verses, with two rhymes variously combined.

Sextina (Italian *sestina*): poem consisting of six stanzas of six hendecasyllables each, and a three-line envoy. No rhyme within one stanza, but the same six rhyme words must be repeated in each, rotating in a prescribed order. Two rhyme words per line in the envoy (e.g. *FDE*, 181–3). The double *sextina* permutates the same six rhyme words twice over in twelve stanzas (*MOA*, 202–4).

Silva: the Spanish name for the free *canzona* stanza: heptasyllables and hendecasyllables, arranged and rhyming at poet's discretion.

Sonnet: the fourteen hendecasyllables of the Italianate sonnet are arranged in two quatrains (*ABBA ABBA*) and two tercets (Variable rhyme scheme, most often *CDE CDE*).

Tercetos (Italian *terza rima*): Rhyme-interlinked stanzas of three hendecasyllables: *ABA, BCB, CDC*, etc.

Villancico: a type of song, being the most common form of gloss, with a refrain and variable number of stanzas. Each stanza subdivided into a main body (usually four lines) and a *vuelta* (return) leading back to the refrain. Usually octosyllabic or hexasyllabic. A typical pattern: *abb* (refrain)-*cddc/cbb* (stanza) (Eg. *LED*, 72).

Good surveys of Castilian versification: D.C. Clarke, "A Chronological Sketch of Castilian Versification," *University of California Publications in Modern Philology*, 34, 3 (Berkeley, 1952), 279–381. R. Baehr, *Manual de versificación española*, translated and adapted by K. Wagner and F. López Estrada (Madrid, Gredos, 1970) [Original: *Spanische Verslehre auf historischer Grundlage* (Tübingen, Max Niemeyer, 1962)].

Abbreviations

Periodicals:
BHS, Bulletin of Hispanic Studies.
BRAE, Boletín de la Real Academia Española.
HR, Hispanic Review.
MLN, Modern Language Notes.
NRFH, Nueva Revista de Filología Hispánica.
PMLA, Publications of the Modern Language Association of America.
RFE, Revista de Filología Española.
RR, Romanic Review.
Books:
Primary Sources:
AVG, see Cervantes, Avalle-Arce ed.
FDE, see Gil Polo, Ferreres ed.
LED, see Montemayor, López Estrada ed.
MOA, See Lope de Vega, Morby ed.
NBAE, 7, see Montemayor, Gálvez de Montalvo, and Gil Polo (Primary Sources, Bibliography), and Menéndez Pelayo (Secondary Sources, Bibliography).
Secondary Sources:
Estudio: López Estrada, *La "Galatea" de Cervantes. Estudio crítico.*
GEO: Osuna, *La Arcadia de Lope de Vega. Génesis, estructura y originalidad.*
Golden Age: R.O. Jones, *A Literary History of Spain: The Golden Age:*
LPE: López Estrada, *Los libros de pastores.*
NPE: Avalle-Arce, *La novela pastoril española.*
Orígenes, II: Menéndez Pelayo, *Orígenes de la novela* (Buenos Aires, 1946), Vol. II
Relaciones: Fucilla, *Relaciones hispanoitalianas.*
SPR: Rennert, *Spanish Pastoral Romances.*

Notes and References

(For details of references given by author's name or abbreviated title only, see Bibliography).

Preface

1. In his first novel *The Golden Fountain* (1870).
2. *Bulletin of Spanish Studies*, 4 (1927), 117–26 and 180–6.
3. See Bibliography for details of all these.

Chapter One

1. See W. Empson, *Some Versions of Pastoral* (London, 1950); P. V. Marinelli, *Pastoral* (London, 1971); R. Poggioli, *The Oaten Flute* (Cambridge, Mass., 1975).
2. See R. Curtius, *European Literature and the Latin Middle Ages* (London, 1953), ch. 10.
3. Together with Apuleius' Latin *Golden Age* (2nd century A.D.), which is not relevant here.
4. For instance, *Apollonius of Tyre* which survived in a fifth or sixth century Latin translation, was translated into many languages, and eventually furnished the material for Shakespeare's *Pericles*.
5. As he wrote in his introduction to *Fiammetta*.
6. Scherillo, *Arcadia di Jacobo Sannazaro* (Turin, 1888), CII.
7. Suggested maybe by Dante's *Vita Nuova*.
8. Scherillo, Introduction, esp. LI-LXXXVI.
9. Scherillo, CLVI.
10. By Tommaso Porcacchi in 1556, by Francesco Sansovino in 1559, and by Giambattista Massarengo in 1596.
11. Especially until the ordinance of 1559, inspired by Counter-Reformation zeal, forbade Spaniards to study abroad, but also afterwards, since its enforcement was fraught with difficulties.
12. See J. H. Elliot, *Imperial Spain: 1469–1716* (London, 1963), esp. ch. IV; and *Spain, A Companion to Spanish Studies* (London, 1973), ed. by P. E. Russell, chs. 4 and 8.
13. See *Golden Age*, ch. 2; B. Gicovate, *Garcilaso de la Vega* (New York, 1975); A. Meozzi, "Lirica della Rinascita italiana nel primo Rinascimento di

Spagna," *Rinascita*, 3 (1940), 345–85. The indispensable modern edition of Garcilaso de la Vega is by E. L. Rivers, *Obras completas* (Madrid, 1964).
14. See R. Reyes Cano, *La Arcadia de Sannazaro en España* (Sevilla, 1973); V. Bocchetta, *Sannazaro en Garcilaso* (Madrid, 1976); Marie A. Z. Wellington, Sannazaro's influence on the Spanish Pastoral Novel, unpublished doctoral thesis (Evanston, Ill., Northwestern University, 1951).
15. See Ch. E. Kany, *The Beginnings of the Epistolary Novel in France, Italy and Spain* (Berkeley, 1937); K. Whinnom, *Diego de San Pedro* (New York, 1974).
16. H. Thomas, *Spanish and Portuguese Romances of Chivalry* (Cambridge, 1920), p. 147.
17. Which had been readily accessible from the beginning of the century to all those, and they were many in cultured circles, who were able to read Italian. From 1547 it also became available to the general reading public in a Spanish translation which was reprinted at least four times within the next three decades. In addition, there exist no less than three other complete sixteenth-century translations in manuscript form.
18. *La Arcadia de Sannazaro.*, p. 145.
19. As well-known examples, see the delightful *serranillas* of the Marquess of Santillana (1398–1458).
20. See E. M. Wilson and D. Moir, *The Golden Age: Drama 1492–1700*, (London/New York, 1971), ch. 1; J. P. W. Crawford, *The Spanish Pastoral Drama* (Philadelphia, 1915).
21. See *LPE*. ch. VI; S.P. Cravens, *Feliciano de Silva y los antecedentes de la novela pastoril en sus libros de caballerías* (Chapel Hill, N.C., 1976).
22. Pastoral episodes and themes were beginning to emerge in all kinds of literature, in addition to romances of chivalry and adventure. To mention two well-known examples: Antonio de Torquemada's miscellany *Coloquios satíricos* (1553) includes a miniature pastoral novel and a treatment of the theme of the superiority of country life (mod. ed. in *NBAE*, 7); Antonio de Villegas' *Inventario*, another miscellany (published in 1565 but essentially completed by 1551) contains *Ausencia y soledad de amor* (mod.ed. by López Estrada, see Bibliography), which combines elements from the sentimental novel with a brief pastoral love scene in prose and verse. It is interesting that this same miscellany also includes an early version of the Moorish tale *El Abencerraje* which, although nonpastoral, was frequently interpolated at the end of Book IV of Montemayor's *Diana* from 1561 onward. (See chapter 2, note 10).
23. See Moreno Báez, introduction to *Los siete libros de la Diana*; D.H. Darst, "Renaissance Platonism and the Spanish Pastoral Novel," *Hispania*, Kansas, 52 (1969), 384–92.
24. See P.O. Kristeller, *Eight Philosophers of the Italian Renaissance* (London, 1965; California, 1966).
25. See J.C. Nelson, *Renaissance Theory of Love* (New York, 1958), ch. II.
26. Ficino's own translation into Italian of the commentary was not published until 1544.

27. Translated no less than three times into Spanish: 1568, 1584, and (the best known) in 1590 by Garcilaso de la Vega "El Inca" (Repr. by Menéndez Pelayo in *NBAE*, 21—see Menéndez Pelayo in Bibliography, Secondary Sources.)

28. Written perhaps as much as thirty years before.

29. It was translated into Spanish by Juan Boscán in 1534, and into English in 1561 by Sir Thomas Hoby.

30. P.O. Kristeller, *The Philosophy of Marsilio Ficino* (New York, 1943), pp. 263–68.

31. *Il Cortegiano*, ed. V. Cian (Florence, 1947), 470–95. (In English: *Castiglione, The Book of the Courtier*, translated and introduced by G. Bull (Harmondsworth: Penguin Books, 1976), pp. 323–42).

32. "The image of painting is Ficino's most frequent metaphor. He was himself on close terms with the Pollaiuolo brothers and closely directed the painting of Botticelli's *Primavera*." *The Letters of Marsilio Ficino I* (London, Shepheard Walwyn, 1975), p. 20.

33. Darst, p. 384. See note 23.

34. On the Neoplatonic concept of the harmony between man and nature, see A. A. Parker, *"Theme and Imagery in Garcilaso's first eclogue,"* *BHS*, 25 (1948), 222–27.

Chapter Two

1. Text: All references to *LED*. Biography: Schönherr, *Orígenes* II, *LED*.

2. The traditional date of 26 February 1561 is unconfirmed, but he was definitely dead by December 1562.

3. See T. Fitzmaurice-Kelly, "The Bibliography of the 'Diana enamorada' ", *Revue Hispanique*, 2 (1895), 304–11; H. D. Purcell, "The Date of First Publication of Montemayor's *Diana*," HR, 35 (1967), 364–65.

4. E.g., he confuses Penelope and Medea (*LED*, 177).

5. The literary theorist Sánchez de Lima, in 1580, praised his "very great natural disposition" (*LED*, XXXVIII). Even his pedantic continuator Pérez, while regretting his lack of humanities, acknowledged "his facility in composition, the sweetness of his verse, and his subtle use of words" (Introduction to Pérez's *Diana*).

6. Yong's translation, p. 10 (see Bibliography).

7. No. 36 in Part II of Bandello's collection *Le Novelle*. On Shakespeare and Montemayor, see ch. 7 below.

8. Beginning with the Valladolid 1561 edition of *Diana*, a short story was often interpolated at this point which is neither pastoral nor by Montemayor, but an Andalusian Moorish tale of war and love. The interpolation was doubtless inspired by the commercial expediency of issuing two best sellers under one cover.

9. "The *Diana* of Montemayor: Revaluation and Interpretation" (see Bibliography).

10. The "quest" motif has deep roots in folk literature. See analysis of its use in *Diana* in *NPE*, p. 85.

11. Yong's translation, p. 10.

12. *LED*, LXXII.

13. See A. Solé-Leris, "The Theory of Love in the Two *Dianas*."

14. On courtly love and *Cancioneros*, see A.D. Deyermond, *A Literary History of Spain: The Middle Ages* (London/New York, 1971), pp. 12–14 and 178–200.

15. *NPE*, pp. 85–8.

16. Quotations from J.R. Jones, "Human Time in *La Diana*," pp. 142, 145.

17. The magic potion is most probably derived from Sannazaro's reference (*Prosa nona*) to "il fonte di Cupidine [in Greece] del quale chiunque beve, depone subitamente ogni amore." Sannazaro's source was Pliny's *Natural History*.

18. López Estrada adumbrated: "The water may be an allegory of time" (Introduction to abridged school edition of *Diana* [Saragossa, 1965], p. 15). J.R. Jones, *op.cit*., demonstrated the point in 1968. For related views see: G. Correa, "El templo de Diana en la novela de Montemayor" (1961), suggesting that the potion acts like an accelerated sleeping cure, and C.B. Johnson, "Montemayor's *Diana*: A Novel Pastoral" (1971), comparing Felicia's treatment to lysergic acid psychotherapy, and stressing that "there is at least some medical justification for the philtre."

19. E.g., the opening of Book III.

20. A few more particulars are occasionally given for Diana (*LED*, 23–4, 240–1, 279), but even then it is her attitude and behavior, revealing her state of mind, rather than her appearance that are described.

21. E.g., Selvagia's home is on the Duero, Felismena is from Andalusia, her brother goes to Portugal, Arsileo has studied at Salamanca, and most of Book VII takes place in Montemayor's native valley.

22. M. J. Bayo, *Virgilio y la pastoral española del Renacimiento*, p. 242.

23. *Orígenes* II, p. 196. On Montemayor's syntax and vocabulary, see Moreno Báez, Introduction to *Diana* ed., XLVII-LII, and M. Dêbax, *Léxique de la Diana de Jorge de Montemayor* (Toulouse, 1971).

24. See the illuminating analysis in Moreno Báez, op.cit., XXXVIII-XLI.

25. See *Appendix on Versification*.

26. Probably inspired by Vásquez's poem in praise of Neapolitan court ladies in the *Cancionero General* (2nd ed., 1514). The device became fashionable and was often imitated.

27. His debt to Garcilaso is generally acknowledged, but has not been studied in detail. See, however, Bayo, p. 243, and Moreno Báez, XLVI.

Chapter Three

1. Text: All refs. to *FDE*. Biography: *Orígenes* II, *FDE*.

2. A. Prieto, *Morfología de la novela* (Barcelona, 1975), ch.III.

3. See A. Solé-Leris, "Psychological Realism in the Pastoral Novel: Gil Polo's *Diana Enamorada.*"

4. It dies hard. Even Ferreres still writes that Gil Polo "merely gives a clear sequel to the unfinished adventures," and that Felicia heals the lovers "with her miraculous philtres" *(FDE*, XXIX). Yet as early as 1938, M. Casella had written: "It is not a continuation except in the names of the protagonists" *(Cervantes, Il Chisciotte* [Florence, 1938], I, p. 428).

5. *Golden Age*, p. 61.

6. Montemayor had taken over the standard interpretation of Cupid and his attributes (symbolizing the overriding power of love) as he found it in Leone Ebreo. In Gil Polo's opposite formulation, the god of love "is feigned by vain minds, followed by dishonest wills, and kept in the memories of unoccupied and idle men" *(FDE*, 26).

7. Which was later cut out in all editions from 1577, no doubt as being overly moralistic.

8. *NPE*, pp. 119–23.

9. Going back as far as Posidonius (c.135–c.51 B.C.) who brought many Platonic elements into Stoicism. There was, however, a sharp distinction in metaphysics, as Stoics rejected the doctrine of Ideas.

10. See *Golden Age*, pp.62–3, and R. O. Jones, "Bembo, Gil Polo, Garcilaso: Three Accounts of Love."

11. *Cervantes, Il Chisciotte*, I, p. 428.

12. *NPE*, p. 125.

13. It follows step by step the episode of Cnemon and his stepmother Demaenete in Book I of Heliodorus. The borrowing was already identified in 1625 by Kaspar von Barth, Gil Polo's Latin translator.

14. *LED*, p. 163; *FDE*, p. 172.

15. The "praise of Valencia" passages in Book III are no exception. In spite of the "freshness and naturalness" which some critics claim for them (e.g., *Orígenes* II, 215), they are in fact purely conventional exercises. The sonnet is entirely unspecific, *(FDE*, p.122) and the prose passage (p. 143) has sources in Sannazaro *(Prosa* XI) and in the thirteenth-century Spanish *Crónica General (Relaciones*, pp.68–9; Bayo, p. 263).

16. E.g., *FDE* pp. 38, 78, 107, 118, 180, 191.

17. In the village, Marcelio is ledged, not in Diana's house (though he is her guest) but with "a cousin of Delio's"*(FDE*, p. 71), since her husband is away. In Felicia's palace, it is specified that Diana and Ismenia share a room; Marcelio is lodged next door, and in the morning Diana wakes him by banging on the wall (p. 180), and *not* on the door, to avoid the slightest propinquity.

18. *Orígenes* II, pp. 213, 223.

19. *FDE*, XXXII-XXXV.

20. Bayo, p. 252.

21. See *Appendix on Versification*.

22. R. Ferreres, "Estructura de las canciones de Gil Polo," *RFE*, 43

(1960), 429–37; E. Segura Covarsi, *La canción petrarquista en la lírica española del Siglo de Oro* (Madrid,1949), pp. 132–4, 258–9; Bayo, pp. 251–67.

23. Bayo, pp. 252, 266, 278 n13.

24. For the ideological relationship between Garcilaso and Gil Polo, and their common debt to Bembo, see R.O. Jones, "Bembo, Gil Polo, Garcilaso. Three accounts of love."

25. *Golden Age,* p. 61.

Chapter Four

1. Text: All references are to AVG. Biography: Entwistle.

2. The fundamental study is by López Estrada: *Estudio.*

3. See K.P. Allen, "Cervantes' *Galatea* and the *Discorso intorno al comporre dei Romanzi* of Giraldi Cinthio" for an instructive study of Cervantes' technique of interlinked episodes.

4. "A Matter of Masks: La Galatea."

5. See *Estudio,* pp. 161–2.

6. A theme which was to be developed at length in the inset "Tale of Impertinent Curiosity" in *Don Quixote* (I, chs. 33, 34).

7. See F. López Estrada, "Sobre la Fortuna y el Hado en la literatura pastoril," *BRAE,* 26 (1947), 431–41.

8. E.L. Rivers, "Nature, Art and Science in Renaissance Poetry," p. 257.

9. A. Castro, *El pensamiento de Cervantes* (Barcelona, 1973) updating text of 1st ed. (Madrid, 1925).

10. E.L. Rivers., op. cit., p. 259.

11. E.C. Riley, *Cervantes' Theory of the Novel,* p. 10.

12. Ibid., p. 150.

13. *SPR,* 117; M. Durán, *Cervantes* (New York, 1974), p. 80.

14. See E.C. Riley, " 'El alba bella que las perlas cría'. Dawn-description in the Novels of Cervantes," *BHS,* 33 (1956), 125–37.

15. Material for a study of Cervantes' style: *Estudio,* pp. 121–42; Riley, *Cervantes' Theory of the Novel,* pp. 131–62; E. Náñez, in *Anales cervantinos*: "El diminutivo en *La Galatea*", 2 (1952), 269–85; "El adjetivo en *La Galatea,*" 6 (1957), 133–67; L. Wistén, *Etudes sur le style et la syntaxe de Cervantes* (Lund, 1901, 1906), 2 vols.

16. E.C. Riley, p. 135.

17. E.g., *AVG* I, 22, 30, 67, 103; II, 89, 170, etc.

18. A prime example is the beginning of Elicio's letter to Galatea (*AVG* II, 262). See also *AVG* II, 136–7, 142, 161, 168, etc.

19. See D. Alonso's basic studies "Versos correlativos y retórica tradicional," *RFE,* 28 (1944), 139–53, and "Un aspecto del petrarquismo: la correlación poética" in *Seis calas n la expresión literaria española* by D. Alonso and C. Bousoño (Madrid, 1951).

20. See *Estudio,* pp. 81–109; J.B. Avalle-Arce, *Nuevos deslindes cervanti-*

nos (Barcelona, 1975), ch. V; J.G. Fucilla, *Estudios sobre el petrarquismo en España* (Madrid, 1960); F. López Estrada, "La influencia italiana en *La Galatea* de Cervantes," *Comparative Literature*, 4 (1952), 161–9; A. Raimondi, *Cervantes minore* (Catania, 1914); E. Segura Covarsi, *La canción petrarquista*.

21. Menéndez Pelayo's long unquestioned assumption was proven wrong by López Estrada (*Estudio*, pp. 88–95, 110–14) and G. Stagg ("Plagiarism in *La Galatea*").

22. E.g., *AVG* I, 109, 122, 172, 174, 180; II, 142, 146, 253.

23. "Alma beata et bella" (*Arcadia, Egloga* V).

24. See B. Cinti, introduction to *Galatea* ed. (Turin, 1968); Raimondi, *Cervantes Minore*, op.cit.; M.A.Z. Wellington, "La 'Arcadia' de Sannazaro y 'La Galatea' de Cervantes," *Hispanófila*, 7 (1959), 7–18.

25. *Don Quixote*, I, 6; II, Prologue. Dedications of *Eight Plays and Eight New Interludes* and *Persiles and Sigismunda*.

26. See the excellent analysis in *NPE*, pp. 246–62.

27. See Peter N. Dunn, "Two Classical Myths in *Don Quijote*", *Renaissance and Reformation*, 9 (1972), pp. 2–10.

28. See J. Herrero, "Arcadia's Inferno: Cervantes' attack on pastoral", *BHS*, 55 (1978), pp. 289–99 for a one-sided, but suggestively argued view of the pastoral episodes in *Don Quixote* as an exposure of "the destructive power of the Arcadian dream and of the concept of love which underlies it."

29. *NPE* p. 252.

Chapter Five

1. Text: All references are to *MOA*. Biography: Rennert, Hayes.

2. In *GEO*, the fundamental study. On identification, see pp. 43–118.

3. See J. Scudieri Ruggieri, "Notas a la 'Arcadia' de Lope de Vega," 580–3, and *GEO*, 239–43.

4. *MOA*, 71–9; 134–45; 188–94; 202–10; 251–7; 309–16; 319–23; 324–35; 336–46 and 373–80.

5. *MOA*, 17, 19; *GEO* 231.

6. *NPE*, 162.

7. *GEO*, 236.

8. For examples, see *Golden Age*, 14–15.

9. The classic formulation is by Aulo Giano Parasio in his commentary on Horace's *Art of Poetry* (1531): "poetam rerum omnium peritum esse oportet" (see B. Weinberg, *A History of Literary Criticism in the Italian Renaissance* (Chicago, 1961), I, 97.)

10. This is from Horace's *Ars Poetica* (366): "Mediocrity in poets has never been tolerated by gods, men, or booksellers."

11. The reference is to Ovid's "est deus in nobis" (*MOA*, 268,n.100).

12. *MOA*, 269. Note the shift from *natural-congenital* to *natural-genuine*.

13. *MOA*, 215–17.

14. *MOA*, 421.

15. *GEO*, 162.

16. See K. Whinnom, *Diego de San Pedro* (New York, 1974), on the use of rhetorical devices.

17. On *culteranismo* and its counterpart *conceptismo*, or the cult of literary "wit," see *Golden Age*, pp. 142–5.

18. On Lope's poetry as a whole, see: J.F. Montesinos, *Estudios sobre Lope* (Mexico, 1951 and Salamanca, 1967); D. Alonso, *Poesía española* (Madrid, 1952) and, specifically on *Arcadia*, MOA, 38–40 ,in Spanish. In English, *Golden Age*, pp. 158–61; Hayes, *Lope de Vega*, pp. 81–5.

19. *GEO*, 151.

20. D. Alonso, "Versos correlativos y retórica tradicional", *RFE*, 28 (1944), 145.

21. See M. Ricciardelli, *L'Arcadia di Jacopo Sannazaro e di Lope de Vega* (Naples, 1966).

22. See *GEO*, 159–216, and *MOA*, 29–33.

23. See J.P.W. Crawford, "The Seven Liberal Arts in Lope de Vega's *Arcadia*," *MLN*, 29 (1914), 192–4.

24. On the madness and death of Marta de Nevares, the death of his son Lope Félix, and the elopement of his daughter Antonia.

25. *GEO*, 81–118.

Chapter Six

1. *SPR* and *NPE* to which this chapter is largely indebted.

2. See Bibliography, Primary Sources.

3. May have been written long before, perhaps as early as 1568/69. See *SPR*, 107; *Relaciones*, 71.

4. *NBAE*, 7, 518a.

5. Fols. lxv-xc of ms. *Las Trecientas de Luys Hurtado Poeta Castellano . . .*, in University Library, Santiago de Compostela (Spain). See Rodriguez-Moniño, *El Poeta Luis Hurtado de Toledo. Noticias biobibliográficas* (Valencia, 1964), also *LPE*, 250–4, 345–51.

6. To this day, Madrid's famous Museo del Prado stands on, and takes its name from, such a site.

7. J. Fucilla, "Bernardo de Balbuena's Siglo de Oro and its Sources," *HR*, 15 (1947), 182–93 (modified Spanish version in *Relaciones*, pp. 77–99).

8. Whose Petrarchan poems had been published in 1578.

9. J. Van Horne, *Bernardo de Balbuena. Biografía y crítica.* (Guadalajara, Mex., 1940), p. 138; *Relaciones*, p. 91.

10. *NPE*, p. 211.

11. *NPE*, p. 212.

12. Taken from the whole traditional range, but with a particular interest in Italian sources (Sannazaro, Tasso's *Aminta*, and Guarini's *Pastor Fido*). See Wellington, *"La Constante Amarilis* and its Italian Pastoral Sources," *Philological Quarterly*, 34 (1955), 81–7.

13. *NPE*, p. 218.

14. In *El Passagero* (*The Passenger*) (Madrid: Sánchez, 1617; ed. R. Selden Rose, Madrid, 1914), p. 114.

15. See *NPE*, p. 219.

16. W. F. King, *Prosa Novelistica y academias literarias en el siglo XVII* (Madrid, 1963), p. 150.

17. The plagiarism is analyzed in detail in *NPE*, pp. 132–5.

18. *NPE*, p. 130.

19. M. Alvar, *Estudios sobre el "Octavario" de Doña Ana Abarca de Bolea* (Saragossa, 1945); W.F. King, *op.cit.*, pp. 121–3.

20. *Golden Age*, p. 87.

21. See B.W. Wardropper, *Historia de la poesía lírica a lo divino en la cristiandad occidental* (History of Divinized Lyric Poetry in Western Christendom): Madrid, 1958.

22. Granada, 1575. This not entirely insensitive effort was read with appreciation by St. John of the Cross, and evidently met with some success; a second edition followed within two years.

23. Prologue to *Clear Diana* (see *LED*, XXXIV).

24. For abridged modern ed., see Primary Bibliography. Good brief analysis by E. Anderson Imbert, *Critica interna* (Madrid, 1960), pp. 19–37.

25. For which Cervantes may be partly responsible. In the *Voyage to Parnassus*, he referred to *Las Habidas*—which he ridiculed—as "a book in prose and verse," an indication that he had probably never actually handled it.

26. *SPR*, p. 92.

27. *NPE*, p. 11.

28. *NPE*, p. 227.

29. *SPR*, p. 191; *NPE*, p. 11.

30. It has been customary to refer to a *First Part* published in Ecija in 1638. However, the existence of this has not, to our knowledge, been established. On the other hand, the ecclesiastical approval of the known *Second Part* is dated "Ecija, 3rd January 1638." This suggests that a confusion may have arisen owing to the wording of the title, and that there may, in fact, exist only *one* book, that of Valencia, 1644. (See B.J. Gallardo, *Ensayo de una biblioteca española de libros raros y curiosos*, (Tentative Spanish Bibliography of Rare and Curious Books) II (Madrid, 1866), cols. 50–51.)

31. As described by the ecclesiastical censor in 1638.

32. *Prosa Novelistica*, p. 147.

Chapter Seven

1. For these and other specimens of criticism, see W. Kraus, "Die Kritik des Siglo de Oro am Ritter-und Schäferroman," in *Homenatge a Antoni Rubió i Lluch*, I (Barcelona, 1936), 225–46.

2. Montemayor's *Diana* was on the Index for Portugal from 1581 to 1624,

but never on the Spanish Index, and some references to "fortune" and "fate" were expunged from the 2nd edition of *Galatea* (Lisbon, 1590).

3. R. G. Keightley, "Narrative Perspectives in Spanish Pastoral Fiction."

4. Ibid., p. 194.

5. *LED*, LXXXVII–CI

6. Pérez: seventeen Spanish editions, of which twelve together with Montemayor, and twelve translations (French, English, German), all with Montemayor. Gil Polo: seven Spanish editions (one with Montemayor), eleven translations (French, English, German), all with Montemayor and Pérez and, curiously, a Latin translation by Kaspar von Barth (Hanau, 1625).

7. J. N. Kennedy, introduction, to Yong, *Diana*, xxxiii.

8. For useful summaries, see: France: M. I. Gerhardt, *La Pastorale* (Assen, 1950), G. Reynier, *Le roman sentimental avant l'Astrée* (Paris, 1908); England: J.N. Kennedy, *op.cit.*; Germany: G. Hoffmeister, *Die spanische Diana in Deutschland* (Berlin, 1972).

9. For discussion, see Kennedy, xlvii–lii

10. P. Savj-Lopez, as quoted in Durán, *Cervantes* (New York, 1974), p. 87.

11. I.e., leaving aside the "divinized" versions, and marginal works.

Selected Bibliography

PRIMARY SOURCES

Texts existing in editions since 1900, and summary information on translations. For further bibliographical data see *NPE*, *SPR*, W.F. King, and as indicated in notes and references.

BRAMÓN, FRANCISCO. *Los sirgueros de la Virgen sin original pecado*. (Mexico: 1620. Abridged ed. A. Yáñez (Mexico: Universidad Nacional Autónoma, 1944). Omits most of poetry and dogmatic matter.

CERVANTES SAAVEDRA, MIGUEL DE. *Primera Parte de la Galatea dividida en Seys Libros*. Alcalá de Henares: Juan Gracián, 1585. Editions by (1) R. Schevill and A. Bonilla (Madrid: Bernardo Rodriguez, 1914). Original spelling. (2) J. B. Avalle-Arce (Madrid; Espasa-Calpe, 1961; 2nd ed. 1968) Spelling modernized. Abbreviated. *AVG*. *Translations*: English: G.W.J. Gyll, *Galatea: A pastoral romance* (London, 1867; repr. 1892), very poor; H. Celsner and A.B. Welford, *Galatea* (Glasgow: Gowans and Gray, 1903); Vol. II of *The Complete Works of Miguel de Cervantes Saavedra*, edited and introduced by James Fitzmaurice-Kelly (source for editions and translations). French: adaptation by J.P. Claris de Florian (1783), a prettified travesty, much abridged and with a happy ending, but very popular, reprinted many times, and itself translated into several languages, including into Spanish by C. Pellicer (1797). German: P. Sigismund (Zwickau, 1830); A Keller and P. Notter (Stuttgart, 1840); P.M. Duttenhofer (Stuttgart, 1841). Italian: B. Cinti (Turin, Mursia, 1968) with good introduction and notes.

CORRAL, GABRIEL DE. *La Cintia de Araniuez, Prosas y Versos*. Madrid: Alonso Pérez, 1629. Ed. by J. de Entrambasaguas (Madrid: CSIC, 1629). No introduction, original spelling.

GÁLVEZ DE MONTALVO, LUIS. *El Pastor de Fílida*. Madrid: 1582. Reprint by Menéndez Pelayo in *NBAE*, 7 (See Secondary Sources).

GIL POLO, GASPAR. *Primera Parte de Diana enamorada, cinco libros que prosiguen los siete de la Diana de Jorge de Montemayor*. Valencia: Joan Mey, 1564. Eds. by (1) M. Menéndez Pelayo (*NBAE*, 7, 1907). (2) A. del Saz (Madrid: Ciap, 1929). (3) R. Ferreres (Madrid: Espasa-Calpe, 1953, and reprints). Spelling modernized. Abbreviated FDE. (4) R.L. and M.B. Grismer (Minneapolis, 1959), together with Bartholomew Yong's translation, notes, and glossary. *Translations*: English: see Yong below. French: G. Chappuys (1582, repr. 1587, 1592); A. de Vitray (1623); A.

Rémy (1624, 1625). German: G. Ph. Harsdörfer (1646, 1661, 1663), facsimile: Darmstadt, 1969; Latin: Kaspar von Barth, *Erotodidascalus, sive Nemoralium Libri V* (Hanau, 1625). see *FDE*, XLVI-XLVII, and *LED*, C-CI.

MERCADER, GASPAR. *El Prado de Valencia*. Valencia: Pedro Patricio Mey, 1600. Ed. by H. Mérimée (Toulouse, Bibliotheque Méridionale XI, 1907), with comprehensive introduction.

MONTEMAYOR, JORGE DE. *Los siete libros de la Diana*. Valencia: 1559?. Eds. by (1) Menéndez Pelayo (*NBAE*, 7, 1907) (2) F. López Estrada (Madrid: Espasa-Calpe, 1946, 2nd ed. 1954). Uses text of Barcelona 1561 ed. Spelling modernized. Abbreviated *LED*. (3) E. Moreno Báez, 1st (Madrid: Real Academia Española, 1955), 2nd, revised, and updated bibliography (Madrid: Editora Nacional, 1976). Uses Valencia 1559? text. *Translations*: English: (1) Thomas Wilson (1596), only Book I extant, printed by H. Thomas, *Revue Hispanique*, 50 (1920), 367–418, (2) see Yong below. French: N. Colin (1578, reprint 1579, 1582, 1587, 1592); G. Chappuys (1582); S. G. Pavillon (1582, 1603, 1611, 1612, 1613); J.B. Bertranet (1611, 1613) [Pavillon's and Bertranet's are bilingual Spanish-French eds.]; A. Vitray (1623, 1631); A. Rémy (1624, 1625); Mme. Guillot de Saintonge (1655, 1699, 1733); Le Vayer de Marsilly (1735). German: H.L. von Kuffstein (1619, 1624, 1690); G.Ph. Harsdörfer, revision of Kuffstein's text (1646, 1661, 1663); anon., based on a French translation (1750). Dutch: anon. (1652). Portuguese: A. Lopes Vieira, abridged, with introduction (1924). See *LED*, XCIV-CII.

PÉREZ, ALONSO. *Segunda Parte de la Diana de Montemayor*. Valencia: 1563. *Translations*: English: see Yong below. French (16th cent.) and German (17th cent.): several, always together with Montemayor's *Diana* (see *LED*, XCVIII-CI).

SUÁREZ DE FIGUEROA, CRISTÓBAL. *La Constante Amarilis. Prosas y Versos*. Valencia: Junto al molino de Rouella, 1609. *Translation*: French, N. Lancelot (1614), bilingual Spanish-French.

VEGA CARPIO, LOPE FELIX DE. *Arcadia, prosas y versos . . . Con una exposicion de los nombres Historicos, y Poeticos*. Madrid: Luis Sanchez, 1598. Eds. by (1) L. Guarner (Madrid: Bergua, 1935), *Novelas*, I; (2) F. Sainz de Robles (Madrid: Aguilar, 1964), *Obras escogidas*, II. (3) J. de Entrambasaguas (Madrid, CSIC, 1965), *Obras completas*, I: palaeographic text of *ed. princeps*. (4) E.S. Morby (Madrid: Castalia, 1975). Spelling modernized. Abbreviated *MOA*. *Translation*: French, by N. Lancelot (1624). _____*Pastores de Belén, Prosas y versos divinos*. Madrid: Juan de la Cuesta, 1612. Ed. by S.F. Ramírez (Madrid: Compañía Ibero-Americana de Publicaciones, 1930).

VILLEGAS, ANTONIO DE. *Ausencia y soledad de amor*. Included in *Inventario*. Medina del Campo: 1565. Ed. with introduction by F. López Estrada, *BRAE*, 29 (1949), 99–133.

YONG, BARTHOLOMEW. *Diana of George of Montemayor*. London: Edm.

Bollifant, 1598. Three *Dianas*—Montemayor's, Pérez's and Gil Polo's—
were included under the one title, Gil Polo without the original prelimi-
naries, and with an alternative dedication. Ed. by Judith M.
Kennedy (omitting Pérez): *A Critical Edition of Yong's Translations of George of
Montemayor's DIANA and Gil Polo's ENAMOURED DIANA*. Oxford:
Clarendon Press, 1968. Good introduction and notes.

SECONDARY SOURCES

ALLEN, K.P. "Cervantes' *Galatea* and the *Discorso intorno al comporre dei
Romanzi* of Giraldi Cinthio", *Revista Hispánica Moderna*, 39 (1976–77),
pp. 52–68. Enlightening on Cervantes' structural techniques. Case for
Giraldi as a specific source of literary theories is however difficult to
substantiate.

AVALLE-ARCE, J.B. *La novela pastoril española*. Eds. 1st, Madrid: Revista de
Occidente, 1959; 2nd, updated, Madrid; Istmo, 1974. The fundamental
study by a major scholar in this field. Indispensable. Abbreviated *NPE*.

———Introduction to *AVG (1961, 1968)*. Summarizes views formulated
more fully in *NPE*.

BAYO, M.J. *Virgilio y la pastoral española del Renacimiento*. Madrid: Gredos, 1959. Virgil's influence studied through stylistic analysis of copious
examples.

CASALDUERO, J. "La Galatea," in *Suma cervantina*. Ed. J.B. Avalle-Arce and
E.C. Riley. London: Támesis, 1973. pp. 27–46. Interpretation as "re-
newal of the myth" by giving Galatea a human dimension. Wilful, but
some useful insights.

CORREA, G. "El templo de Diana en la novela de Jorge de Montemayor."
Thesaurus (Bogotá), 16 (1961), 59–76. The lovers' quest as a pursuit of
self-improvement seen in heroic dimensions through the meeting of
natural and supernatural (Felicia). Important.

DARST, DAVID H. "Renaissance Platonism and the Spanish Pastoral Novel."
Hispania, 52 (1969), 384–92. With special reference to Montemayor, Gil
Polo, Cervantes, and Lope de Vega. A valuable study.

EL SAFFAR, RUTH. "Structural and Thematic Discontinuity in Montemayor's
Diana." *MLN*, 86 (1971), 182–98. *Diana* as Montemayor's failed attempt
to resolve a personal love problem. Opinionated and unconvincing.

EMPSON, W. *Some Versions of Pastoral*. London: Chatto + Windus, 1968 (1st
ed. 1935). Pastoral as "the process of putting the complex into the
simple." Its modern equivalents. Idiosyncratic but stimulating.

ENTWISTLE, W. *Cervantes*. Oxford: Clarendon Press, 1940. Perceptive and
balanced biography. Good on pastoral.

FERRERES, R. Introduction to Gil Polo's *Primera Parte de Diana enamorada*.
Madrid: Espasa-Calpe, 1953. *(FDE)* Useful general introduction and
notes. Bibliography of editions and translations.

FUCILLA, J. G. *Relaciones hispanoitalianas*. Madrid: *RFE* Anejo LIX, 1953.
Includes identifications of Sannazaro imitations in Gil Polo, Gálvez de

164 THE SPANISH PASTORAL NOVEL

Montalvo, Cervantes, and Balbuena. Useful, though often overstated. Abbreviated *Relaciones*.

GERHARDT, MIA I. *La Pastorale. Essai d'Analyse Littéraire*. Assen: Van Gorcum, 1950. Pastoral poetry, prose, and drama in Italy, Spain, and France to the end of seventeenth century. Painstaking and not unperceptive, but vitiated by reliance on a nineteenth-century conception of "realism" as critical yardstick. Less than adequate on Spanish pastoral novels.

HAYES, FRANCIS C. *Lope de Vega*. New York: Twayne, 1967. Survey of life and works, with notes and bibliography.

JOHNSON, C. B. "Montemayor's *Diana*: A Novel Pastoral." *BHS*, 48 (1971), 20–35. Suggestive study of how lyrical and narrative elements combine in a new kind of pastoral. Important.

JOHNSON, L. DEUTSCH. "Three who made a revolution: Cervantes, Galatea and Calíope." *Hispanófila*, 19 (1976), 23–33. Calliope as ordainer of a revolution to save poetry and the pastoral myth. Stimulating but strained.

JONES, J.R. "Human Time in *La Diana*." *Romance Notes*, 10 (1968), 139–46. The significance of time in Montemayor. Essential.

JONES, R. O. "Bembo, Gil Polo, Garcilaso: Three accounts of love." *Revue de Littérature Comparée*, 40 (1966), 526–40. Gil Polo's debt to Bembo, and similarities with Garcilaso's ideology. Valuable.

———*A Literary History of Spain. The Golden Age: Prose and Poetry. The Sixteenth and Seventeenth Centuries*. London: Ernest Benn/New York: Barnes + Noble, 1971. The best one-volume survey of the period. Balanced and illuminating. See especially chs. 1 and 2 on the Renaissance in Spain; ch. 3 on sixteenth-century prose fiction, and ch. 5 on sixteenth-century poetry after Garcilaso. Abbreviated *Golden Age*.

KEIGHTLEY, R.G. "Narrative perspectives in Spanish pastoral fiction." *AUMLA* (Queensland), 4 (1975), 194–219. Valuable study of narrative techniques in Montemayor, Gil Polo, and Cervantes.

KING, W.F. *Prosa novelística y academias literarias en el siglo XVII*. Madrid: Real Academia Española, 1963. Influence of literary academies on novel-writing in seventeenth century. Useful information on the later pastoral novels.

LÓPEZ ESTRADA, F. *La "Galatea" de Cervantes, Estudio crítico*. La Laguna de Tenerife: Universidad de la Laguna, 1948. The indispensable starting-point for any study of *Galatea*. Abbreviated *Estudio*.

———Introduction to Montemayor's *Los siete libros de la Diana*. Madrid: Espasa-Calpe, 1946, 1954 (*LED*). A mine of literary, biographical and bibliographical information (with bibliography of editions and translations). Copious notes.

———*Los libros de pastores en la literatura española, La órbita previa*. Madrid: Gredos, 1974. Vol. I of a monumental work. Comprehensive analysis of pastoral tradition and all other elements that contributed to the Spanish pastoral romances. Essential. (Vol. II, on the novels, to follow). Abbreviated *LPE*.

Lowe, Jennifer. *"The Cuestión de Amor and Cervantes' Galatea." BHS*, 43 (1966), 98–108. Analysis of Galatea's structure in terms of the literary tradition of presentation of "love cases."

Marinelli, P.V. *Pastoral*. London: Methuen, 1971. Good introduction to mental world of pastoral. Concerned primarily with English literature. Suggests child-cult is modern version of pastoral.

Menéndez Pelayo, M. *Orígenes de la novela*. Madrid: Bailly-Baillière, 1905–15. 4 vols. in *Nueva Biblioteca de Autores Españoles* series (*NBAE*). Vol. I (*NBAE*, 1, 1905) includes studies on romances of chivalry, sentimental novels, Greek romances, and pastoral novels. Vol. II (*NBAE*, 7, 1907, repr. 1931) includes editions of Montemayor and Gil Polo (now superseded), and Gálvez de Montalvo. Vol. IV (*NBAE*, 21, 1915) includes "El Inca" Garcilaso's translation of Ebreo's *Dialoghi d'amore*. Critical matter (without texts) reprinted in (1) *Edición Nacional* (Santander, 1962), 4 vols., (2) *Obras Completas* (Buenos Aires: Espasa-Calpe Argentina, 1946), 3 vols.; vol II of this abbreviated *Orígenes,II*. Broad scholarship and wealth of data; views strongly dated. Must still be consulted, but in the light of more recent research.

Morby, E.S. Introduction to Lope de Vega's *Arcadia*. Madrid: Castalia, 1975. (*MOA*). Major contribution to *Arcadia* studies. Copious notes and full bibliography. Essential.

Moreno Báez, E. Introduction to Montemayor's *Los siete libros de la Diana*. Madrid: Real Academia Española, 1955, and Editora Nacional, 1976. See Primary Sources. Lucid outline of Renaissance Neoplatonism, good structural and stylistic analysis. Notes mainly philological, and biographical on *Canto de Orpheo*. Valuable.

Osuna, R. "La crítica y la erudición del siglo XX ante La Galatea." *RR*, 54 (1963), 241–51. Critical summary of research to that date.

———*La Arcadia de Lope de Vega. Génesis, estructura y originalidad*. (Madrid: Anejos Boletín Real Academia Española XXVI, 1973. Substantial, comprehensive and scholarly. Essential. Abbreviated *GEO*.

Perry, T.A. "Ideal Love and Human Reality in Montemayor's *La Diana*." *PMLA*, 84 (1969), 227–34. Perceptive on the fusion of myth and reality; obtuse on use of Leone Ebreo. Suggestive psychological reading of Belisa's episode.

Poggioli, R. *The Oaten Flute. Essays on Pastoral Poetry and the Pastoral Ideal*. Cambridge, Mass: Harvard U.P., 1975. Though its strongly psychological approach has its limitations, this is a major contribution to the revaluation of pastoral.

Rennert, H.A. *The Life of Lope de Vega (1562–1635)*. Glasgow, 1904; reprint New York: Stechert, 1937. Still the standard work in English, but see, if possible, its updated Spanish version: *Vida de Lope de Vega* by A. Castro and H. S. Rennert, 2nd ed. updated by F. Lázaro Carreter (Salamanca, 1968).

————*The Spanish Pastoral Romances*. Philadelphia: University of Pennsylvania, 1912. Final version of study first published in *PMLA*, 7 (1892), 1–119. Strikingly unsympathetic to whole genre yet, until *NPE*, the only attempt at a complete survey, with individual attention to each work and brief (often caricatured!) plot outlines. Critical views entirely dated, but still basic for bio-bibliographical information. Abbreviated *SPR*.

RILEY, E.C. *Cervantes' Theory of the Novel*. Oxford: Clarendon Press, 1962. A classic study. Much of relevance to *Galatea*.

RIVERS, E.L. "Nature, Art and Science in Renaissance Poetry." *BHS*, 44 (1967), 255–66. The best summary of the Renaissance Nature Art dialectic in Spanish letters with brief discussion of *Galatea*.

SCHÖNHERR, J.G. *Jorge de Montemayor, sein Leben und sein Schäferroman. Die "Siete Libros de la Diana."* Halle: Leipzig University, 1886. The pioneer study, now superseded except on biography.

SCUDIERI RUGGIERI, JOLE. "Notas a la *Arcadia* de Lope de Vega." *Cuadernos hispanoamericanos* (Madrid), 54 (1963), 577–605. General review of work and positive critical appraisal.

————"Stilistica e stile nell' *Arcadia* di Lope." *Quaderni Ibero-Americani* (Turin), 31 (1965), 159–81. The only analysis so far of prose style in *Arcadia*. Important.

SOLÉ-LERIS, A. "The theory of Love in the Two *Dianas*: A Contrast" *BHS*, 36 (1959), 65–79. How Montemayor's love theory differs from that of his source, Leone Ebreo. His fatalistic conception contrasted with Gil Polo's stress on reason and free will.

————"Psychological Realism in the Pastoral Novel: Gil Polo's *Diana enamorada*," *BHS*, 39 (1962), 43–7. Psychological motivation and its relevance to the introduction of moral issues.

STAGG, G. "Plagiarism in *La Galatea*," *Filologia Romanza* (Turin), 6, (1959), 255–76. Cervantes' use of Bembo and Equicola as sources; recapitulation of previous research in this field. Essential.

————"A matter of masks: *La Galatea*," in *Hispanic Studies in Honour of J. Manson*. Eds. D.M. Atkinson and A.H. Clarke. Oxford: Dolphin, 1972. pp. 255–67. Most thoughtful contribution to the question of the identity of characters. Essential.

WARDROPPER, B.W. "The *Diana* of Montemayor: Revaluation and Interpretation." *Studies in Philology*, 48 (1951), 126–44. A milestone in the revaluation of pastoral. Essential on significance of pastoral setting, structure of *Diana*, and love theory.

Index